CW01080713

1,000,000 Books

are available to read at

www.ForgottenBooks.com

Read online
Download PDF
Purchase in print

ISBN 978-0-428-76296-4
PIBN 10781423

This book is a reproduction of an important historical work. Forgotten Books uses
state-of-the-art technology to digitally reconstruct the work, preserving the original format
whilst repairing imperfections present in the aged copy. In rare cases, an imperfection in
the original, such as a blemish or missing page, may be replicated in our edition. We do,
however, repair the vast majority of imperfections successfully; any imperfections that
remain are intentionally left to preserve the state of such historical works.

Forgotten Books is a registered trademark of FB &c Ltd.
Copyright © 2018 FB &c Ltd.
FB &c Ltd, Dalton House, 60 Windsor Avenue, London, SW19 2RR.
Company number 08720141. Registered in England and Wales.

For support please visit www.forgottenbooks.com

1 MONTH OF
FREE
READING

at

www.ForgottenBooks.com

By purchasing this book you are eligible for one month membership to ForgottenBooks.com, giving you unlimited access to our entire collection of over 1,000,000 titles via our web site and mobile apps.

To claim your free month visit:

www.forgottenbooks.com/free781423

* Offer is valid for 45 days from date of purchase. Terms and conditions apply.

English
Français
Deutsche
Italiano
Español
Português

www.forgottenbooks.com

Mythology Photography **Fiction**
Fishing Christianity **Art** Cooking
Essays Buddhism Freemasonry
Medicine **Biology** Music **Ancient**
Egypt Evolution Carpentry Physics
Dance Geology **Mathematics** Fitness
Shakespeare **Folklore** Yoga Marketing
Confidence Immortality Biographies
Poetry **Psychology** Witchcraft
Electronics Chemistry History **Law**
Accounting **Philosophy** Anthropology
Alchemy Drama Quantum Mechanics
Atheism Sexual Health **Ancient History**
Entrepreneurship Languages Sport
Paleontology Needlework Islam
Metaphysics Investment Archaeology
Parenting Statistics Criminology
Motivational

STATE OF COLORADO

CITY AND COUNTY OF DENVER

HON. BEN. B. LINDSEY

FATHER OF JUVENILE COURT.

OF DENVER, COLORADO

THE NEW YORK
PUBLIC LIBRARY
615398A
ASTOR, LENOX AND
TILDEN FOUNDATIONS
R   1932   L

THE MERCHANTS PUBLISHING CO.
Makers
Denver,   –   Colorado

FOREWORD

This booklet is prepared by the probation department of the Juvenile Court of the City and County of Denver.

Chapters one, two, three and four are made up almost entirely from the writings of Judge Lindsey on the Juvenile Court laws and work.

Chapter five ("Facts and Figures") and chapter six ("The Court Approved"), together with the charts and photographs, are prepared by the probation officers from the court records, press clippings and letters received by the Court.

The financial statement is prepared by the clerk from the books and the former annual reports. These reports have been issued yearly to show what is being done in this court.

In addition to the ordinary annual report of the court there is added a history and detailed account of its work for Colorado's children for the past three years.

As remarkable as it may seem, because of the fact that the County Court of Denver (which is also the Juvenile Court) is under the fee system in its civil cases—all officers being paid out of fees earned from litigants in civil law suits, and not out of any fund paid by taxpayers—we show by this report that we actually earned and collected in the three years from litigants in the civil division of the County Court sufficient money to pay the salary of the Judge, all the clerks and the probation officers (services of probation officers were voluntary and without pay prior to 1903), and returned to the county over $10,000 cash, so that instead of the taxpayers of the city and county or State paying one cent to save over $270,000 by the work of the Juvenile Court alone in three years, in addition to 95 per cent. of its delinquent children, as shown by this report, *the taxpayers of Denver were actually paid by the Court and received into the county treasury over $10,000 in the doing of this work.*

The Judge had a right as the sole and only authority under the law to use up every cent of this money for extra clerical help, or exorbitant salaries, but the business of the court has been run as nearly as possible as any other business should be, on an economical and reasonable business basis, consistent with every political condition, yet during the same period the people of Colorado have paid over one million of dollars to detect, prosecute and care for criminals from Denver alone. In one year of the same period, the boys brought to the Juvenile Court by officers for offenses have themselves not only been successfully corrected, but in addition thereto have become helpers in the work. Rightly directed, they have turned upon their enemies and helped to smash the *causes*. They have, for instance, prosecuted, convicted and fined or sent to jail through the Juvenile Court (on adult days) more men for violating such laws for the protection of childhood as forbidding the sale of cigarettes, tobacco, liquor, immoral literature, dangerous firearms, etc., and for permitting them to enter saloons and immoral places, than have all the combined forces of the sheriff's and police departments in all the courts in any ten years of Denver's history. And Denver is cleaner and more wholesome in this respect than most cities of its size. It has now, however, a sheriff's and police department sympathizing and working with the Juvenile Court.

The work by the boys has cost practically nothing. Even in the past year when we have had to send only eighteen or twenty, out of several hundred of them, to the State Industrial School, they have without exception received from the Judge their own warrants, taken the train alone and, without the slightest surveillance or suspicion thereof, delivered themselves to the superintendent, returned their own writs, showing its faithful execution, and thus not only saved to the county a large amount of money in mileage fees and services of officers, but to the State of Colorado good friends and citizens of tomorrow. We have asked, by the way, that this money be given to the faithful (bad?) boys, since it was saved from the sheriff.

The work and business of the County Court has more than doubled since Judge Lindsey came to the bench.

On June 1, 1904, an additional and much needed judge was added in the person of Hon. Henry V. Johnson, ex-Mayor of Denver. This will relieve Judge Lindsey of much of the civil business and give him more time for his favorite work with the children's cases.

Necessarily this will add to the expense of the court in the future, but since this court still does a greater volume of business than the District Court, it may be said by way of justification, that with all the new officials occasioned thereby, it will at the same time still occasion only half the expense.

THOMAS L. BONFILS,

Clerk of the County and Juvenile Court of Denver, Colo.

O. S. STORRS,

Chief Probation Officer.

IDA L. GREGORY,

LILBURN MERRILL,

Probation Officers.

THE JUDGE'S ESTIMATE OF THE WORK.

It would be practically impossible to show by a mere report of the text of laws and the numbers of children in court, their disposition, etc., what is meant by the Juvenile Court of Denver. Something of its character, meaning, history and the purpose and spirit back of it all must necessarily be referred to. What has been done must be told just as it was done, in order to be understood and appreciated. This we have attempted in the midst of a busy civil court, and, therefore, necessarily hasty and imperfect. It will be seen that the Juvenile Court rightly understood is something of an effort at man building—character building. It involves constant work, constant effort, constant struggle. It is a strenuous life for those truly enlisted.

I have no apology to make for the weary after court hours and long evenings I have spent with the boys in the court, in chambers, in the jail, in the alleys, in the slums; the struggle in the legislature for laws, for more attendance officers, for public support and sympathy, the misunderstandings, the ignorance, the trials and troubles with officials to enforce laws for the protection of childhood, the fights for nearly everything we have, from the rain baths to the paid probation officers, for they have all come and come to stay. No work of mine for several years upon the bench of an important court has been, in my humble judgment, of half so much importance, though during that time I have had the honor to assist in the revision of all the probate laws of the State and to take part in other important legislation and litigation. Yet I positively disclaim the title of "Father of the Juvenile Court of Colorado," as some of my over-zealous friends have attempted to confer. I have only been a worker in the ranks, and so much, through so many earnest souls, has gone to make up our present system of children's laws that no single individual can well be so credited.

I shall feel more than repaid and honored if I am permitted to humbly stand with those who have really aided the children of the State, of which there can be no nobler service to our country.

TWO BOYS.

I know two boys—brothers. The older came to the criminal court before the days of the Juvenile Court. He is a man to-day and in prison. The younger was equally wayward. He was brought to the Juvenile Court nearly four years ago. He came frightened and terrified, just as the brother had several years before to another tribunal. The officer told me that the boy was an amazing liar. I simply replied that he would probably have been a worse liar under similar conditions. The man felt "sore" and mentally resolved that there would be no use in bringing boys to the Juvenile Court, because the judge did nothing to them, meaning, of course, that I did not send them to jail. Personal work for hours and hours and days with that boy was not his notion of "doing something" to the boy. One day, months after, in a busy civil session of the Court, trying a will case involving two millions of dollars, the court room door opened; the same boy poked in his tousled head and freckled face. The bailiff "shooed" him out, but he returned, not with any thought of disobedience, but because he had learned he also had rights there. I ordered a recess of three minutes, to the disgust, I fear, of one or two of the distinguished counsel, and the boy came to the bench, unafraid and smiling now, where he was crying with fear the first time when he was brought there months before. I prefer a spirit of trust and love to a spirit of fear and hate. You can do more with it in the end. He was what was commonly called a street boy or newsboy. He said that he was having trouble; that for two years the policeman on the beat had let him sell papers on a certain corner, and now, as he expressed it, "a fly guy" had taken his place, and "'cause he was a new cop he thought he owned the town," and had therefore ordered him off the favorite corner and he was losing 50 cents a day. The boy had a case, to me as important as the one before the bar involving the millions that a dead man had left behind for surviving selfishness and cunning craft to do battle in the courts. I do not apologize but I rejoice that I thought the boy and his little cause the most important thing before the court. "What can I do for you, Morris?" said I to the childish petitioner pleading his own cause. "Well," said the boy, who had apparently read papers as well as sold them, "if you will give me an injunction agin dat cop, Judge, I will get my rights." And the kindly clerk, catching the spirit of the thing, handed me an injunction writ, in the body of which I wrote a kindly note to the "fly guy," who was the "new cop." I told him Morris was a good boy, because for three months he had brought splendid reports from his teacher, and for this reason I was his friend and he was mine. I explained to the boy the duties of an officer and how he represented the law and he must respect him. He said the other cop was a good law, but he feared this one was not. With the writ in a sealed envelope he went away rejoicing. In a week he came again with the usual excellent report, and I said: "Well, Morris, how did the injunction work?" "Oh," said he, "I tell yer, Judge, it worked fine, it did. He liked to dropped dead when he read it. Say, Judge, he is trying to be my friend, now; he wants to get on the good side of me. He thinks I've got a pull wid de court." Frequent talks with this boy, interest and assistance of the right kind have made him know rightly and understand. He is a young man, now, working hard, ambitious and proud to do right. He was never in trouble again. He is a good citizen. No matter how critics may theorize as to the effect of such an incident; this is the fact. We cannot say the same for the brother, who was subjected to the jail and the criminal court of the old days, for the State is caring for him.

THE DOCTRINE OF FEAR.

This boy did not cry—he was not afraid in the beginning because he did wrong. He was afraid because he got caught. The ordinary punishment of the jail and criminal law for such boys as a rule does not encourage to do right, to fear to do wrong. It encourages rather to fear to get caught, and too often fills the soul with bitterness, craft and cunning. This boy in the Juvenile Court learned to fear to do wrong because it was wrong and to do right because it was right, not because he might get in jail. I do not believe in the doctrine of fear. It may win in cases, but it is not right in principle. It is a short cut, but a dangerous path. Its winnings are not the permanent or lasting ones. The consequence of wrong-doing is and should be pointed out, but too often the boy gets it into his head that it is only to escape the consequences that he should do right. In any event, if we must have a "bogie man" to frighten and to scare, as we (wrongfully) have hobgoblins for children and demons, fierce avenging gods and dragons for the savage and the heathen, it had better be the consequence of wrong that comes to men in the jail and the penitentiary rather than the Juvenile Court, or even the Industrial School. We want no boy in the Juvenile Court to be afraid of the Court. They are all my friends, even to the last, when they take their own warants and go away alone to the Industrial School, without the guard of any officer, giving up their haunts and the freedom of a city life so dear to the heart of such a boy. Not one has ever failed us.

It is useless to question the wisdom of a thing that has proved successful. The endorsement of the Juvenile Court of Denver by all the people after four years, including the police and detective departments, the special secret service associations, the schools, homes, churches and business men, and the facts and figures stated herein, leave no question that more reform and better results are accomplished by pursuing these principles than the hopeless and too often useless severity of the past. There is, of course, always the question of knowing how and doing the thing. But there is always some one who can and will. Kindness must not be permitted to be mistaken for weakness. You must understand the boy and he must understand you. This is easier said than done.

The personal work is the main thing. It is said that St. Paul, in arming the Christian soldier, placed sincerity and enthusiasm above all things. Thus armed should be the Juvenile Court worker. He or she should have the magnetism of Moses, the patience of Job, the firmness of Abraham, the wisdom of Solomon and the unselfishness and love of our Lord and Master.

If this effort shall help the cause of the Juvenile Court and its kindred laws in behalf of the childhood of this nation, the State of Colorado and those of her citizens who have helped shall be more than gratified, honored and repaid.

LILBURN MERRILL   MRS. IDA L. GREGORY   O. S. STORRS
MASTER FRANK KEMP   THOS. L. BONFILS

OFFICERS OF THE JUVENILE COURT

CHAPTER I

The Fight for Childhood

THE FIGHT FOR CHILDHOOD.

Of course the home, the church and the school with their natural moral and uplifting influences have been responsible in the past, and must continue to be in the future, for the manhood and womanhood of this nation. What is said here is not intended to detract from their importance, but rather to emphasize it. It is because the home sometimes fails, or there is no home, or for causes over which the home has no control, and which the church and school do not reach, or for deficiencies which they are powerless to supply, that auxiliaries to these are sought to be furnished by the State.

We shall show how the State of Colorado is the first and only State thus far that by positive law places the responsibility for the delinquency of the child upon the parent and the home. How parents and other citizens responsible are often fined and sent to jail for the faults of children. We would make some parents do their duty. We would help others who need help. We would improve environment and add to opportunity for good as the best duty of the State to the child.

Children in many States at the age of seven, and in practically all at the age of ten, when violating the laws of the land are amenable, not to the home, the church or the school, but to the State. Then as fathers, mothers or citizens can we occupy ourselves with a more important problem than that of the children? And since the State is placed above the parent and made the judge, as it often is, as to the proper discharge of the parental function; if it may assume it, as it often must, where the parent fails, then at least as great responsibility devolves upon the State as upon the parent to properly discharge its every function, act or duty toward the child, and as wisely and well.

The facts disclosed, however dark, in that phase of the child problem in cities dealt with by the Juvenile Court, can offer no encouragement to the pessimist. A more important fact is the uplifting movements being furnished for childhood betterment all over this country, of which the Juvenile Court is only one.

All the new movements, including the court itself, are educational.   There are the public play grounds, the ungraded
schools, the vacation schools, the manual training and trades
work, the settlements, the boys' clubs, the camps, the fresh
air funds, and (as connected with the Juvenile Court of Denver) the juvenile improvement associations, the little citizens'
leagues for law enforcement, the physical department, the
rain baths, the good literature and other uplifting things too
numerous to mention.   All these tend to prevent delinquency
and crime, and just so far as we extend them, just so far will
we reduce the necessity for juvenile courts or any other courts.
We would be better off, not without them, but without the
necessity for them.

So closely allied are these uplifting movements with the
school, as we formerly understood it, that we must soon cease
(if we have not already) to draw any distinction between them.
In any event they are all embraced under the comprehensive
head of education.

Thus the home, the school and religious influences, supplemented by all the great social agencies that build up a
community, is caring for and protecting the child life of this
nation better than it ever has before.   It is producing the noblest
citizenship the world has even known.

And even as we pity the children of the tenements, or those
that crowd the slums or the congested districts of great cities,
we can rejoice as never before at the ever-increasing army of
willing hands and hearts, zealously anxious to join in the work
of rescue.   And if such sights become distressing there is no
need of misrepresentation.   There is no need for despair or
gloom.   We can always turn with refreshing cheerfulness to
the towns, the villages, the country, and even the greater part
of the city with their millions of wholesome homes and happy
children.   Yet there has been more rejoicing at the return of
the one sheep that was lost, than for the ninety and nine that
went not astray.

These helpful movements should fill us with the live-
liest sort of optimism.   They are really more significant
than the conditions which cause them to spring into being.
The dragon that moved about in the land demanding the rich
blood of youth to satiate its appetite, called forth its St.

"A SNITCHING BEE"
(In the Judge's Chambers)

George. We are coming to regard the great majority of the youthful offenders, especially in our great cities, as the victims of environment, the lack of opportunity for good, often as helpless for what and where they are as the one in the fabled dragon's teeth. And so these great movements for the betterment of our children are simply typical of the noblest spirit of this age, the Christ spirit of unselfish love, of hope and joy. It has reached its acme in what were formerly the criminal courts. The old process is changed. Instead of coming to destroy we come to rescue. Instead of coming to punish we come to uplift. Instead of coming to hate we come to love.

That this is no weak sentiment, no idle dream, nor evidence of leniency, the results of four years in the Juvenile Court of Denver, as well as those of other cities, will fairly show. Nor does it presuppose a lack of firmness, discipline or strength. On the contrary, it has required more firmness and less brutality, more discipline and less retribution, more earnest interest and less indifference, more strength and less ignorant authority than ever before.

YOUTH AND CRIME.

Did you ever inquire how many children are dealt with every year in the criminal courts? Do you care? Are you interested? The kind of country we have and your security and happiness therein depend upon the kind of citizens we have. Then what makes for good or evil citizenship is the thing which should concern us most. We have at least cared in the Juvenile Court. This is the main thing. To think, to know, to care and then to do is better than to remain in indifferent, ignoble ease, doing nothing, even if the something done is not just the right thing. In the end good will come. Error will be overcome, mistakes will be righted, and truth and justice, seasoned with love and mercy, will triumph.

We have at least all worked and worked hard in the Juvenile Court, and we have learned things—often out of the mouths of babes. What this work has been, what it is, whether it is necessary or worth while, may, we trust, be judged from what follows.

For several years the Juvenile Court of Denver has been

supplied by a press clipping bureau from city papers throughout the United States with those items pertaining to juvenile offenders. The result is almost appalling, in fact so great that lest it be misinterpreted into pessimism and our own position misunderstood, we have been constrained to preface this report with a ring of optimism. Yet at the risk of misinterpretation important facts cannot be suppressed. There seems to be no doubt that such offenses, especially in the cities, up to at least the last two years, have been amazingly upon the increase, and it is well to find the fire on the scent of smoke and do all we can to stamp it out before it becomes a conflagration. Thousands of such clippings have been received, and it is not pretended that they represent more than a small part of all. Here are just a few samples of the press and editorial comments, covering a brief period of time, from various cities as they are told under some of the following expressive headlines: "Ten Thousand Boys Arrested Last Year" (referring to one city); "Four Thousand Out of the Sixteen Thousand Arrests Last Year Were Boys Under Twenty" (referring to a city of less than 150,000); "British Prison Commission Reports Criminals Being Generated From Boys"; "Bandits Caught Mere Boys" (this is not uncommon from many cities); "Over Half the Murderers Last Year Mere Boys"; "Boy Burglars Getting Common"; "Thieving Increasing Among Children"; "Gangs Generating Thieves"; "Desperate Boy Bandits Captured, Aged 12, 13 and 15, Respectively."

It seems hardly possible that there are so many murderers who are so young, but as we scan these clippings we find such samples among recent murderers as the Van Wormers of New York, the Biddles of Pennsylvania, the car barn murderers of Illinois, the Collinses of Missouri, the boy murderer of Nebraska, the Youngblood murderers of Denver, the boy train wreckers of the West and the reform school boy murderers of California. And so the list might be multiplied indefinitely, showing the awful chances taken in the misdirected and hot blood of youth. With few exceptions all these have gone to the slaughter house, all in their teens or early twenties, over three-fourths of them formerly in jail for other serious crimes; and still the grind keeps on. These clippings show that instead

WE DON'T CARE WHETHER SCHOOL KEEPS OR NOT

of "mere boys" being added by the headline artists doubtless to indicate an exception, it is becoming quite the contrary.

We recall the case of a young man (and it is one of hundreds) who had been in the criminal court and the police court at the age of thirteen. At the age of twenty he shot down a policeman who was heroically performing his duty. And yet suppose at the age of thirteen that boy had been studied, helped, looked after and carefully handled, at twenty would the policeman be maimed for life or dead, a young wife and child a charge on the community and a strong, robust young man a charge on the State for life? Perhaps not, and even so we could have felt better about it, and in the sight of God less accountability. Was the State responsible? Yes, even more than the boy, for he was in jail; he was in the plastic stage. The State had him in time and it did nothing—not even to try. The State treated him as a man, dealt with him as a man. They had tried in a day to put a man's head on the boy's shoulders, and in attempting to do this tried what God had forbidden. In this the State was foolish. Just as foolish as if it tried at thirteen years of age to raise him to his full stature. Strange that if his money or property was involved he could control none of it; he needed a guardian. But his morals—the boy, the man in embryo, the citizen—needed no guardian. He needed no help. He needed punishment. He needed retribution, and so as a boy he got what men get, that which is often barbarous even for men. I have seen others like that boy in jail. I have seen them eleven to fifteen years of age in the same bullpen with men and women with chains about their waists and limbs. And I have seen them crowded together in idleness, in filthy rooms where suggestiveness fills the mind with all things vile and lewd. Such has too often been the first step taken by the great State in the correction of the child. But the fight against the jail for children in Denver has been fought and won. The wholesome detention school has taken its place, just as better things must take the place of the past methods of the criminal courts in dealing with erring childhood. We are trying, searching for that thing. We shall go on undaunted and undismayed, feeling that it is better, even if misunderstood, even with handicaps, mistakes and seeming failures to strive upward for the cause of the children of the State. Theirs' is a cause. It is a just cause. In the end we shall find what is best, and then will come the final victory—the supreme victory—that is always for God, our country, our brothers and humanity; and there also is the reward to those in the ranks who fight—the supreme satisfaction — the highest and best thing in life, the good that men do for men, and the best service that can be rendered to mankind is when mankind is in the adolescent period of golden influences, the period of childhood when character is plastic and can be moulded for good or evil as clay in the potter's hands.

CHAPTER II

The Law and The Court

THE JUVENILE LAW AND COURT.

The Juvenile Court idea is spreading rapidly all over the United States. There is no better evidence of this than the numerous inquiries constantly received by the officers of this Court. These inquiries have come from nearly every State in the Union, as well as Great Britain and different parts of Europe and Australia. The purpose of this report is to answer these inquiries, to set forth the detailed working of the Colorado Juvenile Laws and the results thereof. It is also prepared by request as a part of the exhibit of the Juvenile Court of Denver at the World's Fair in St. Louis.

PROBATION.

The probation feature of the Juvenile Court is not new. Probation is simply a suspension of a sentence upon conditions imposed by the Court under a system of supervision after release. If these conditions are complied with, and the offender conducts himself properly, and by his own effort overcomes the error or evil into which he has fallen, he is relieved entirely from any penalty. He thus becomes a co-worker with the State. Excellent laws for the probation of children offenders have existed in a number of Western States for more than twenty years.

NEW FEATURES OF LAW.

About the only important new thing that the juvenile law (so-called) undertook to do was to permit the correction of children without their being charged and convicted of what would technically be a crime. This was done by designating all offenders under sixteen years of age as delinquents, and permitting them to be charged as such upon petitions to be filed by any citizen. Yet the powers of the Chancery Courts and the general statutes of many of the States embodied substantially all that was necessary to care for dependent and delinquent children. There is very little that is new in principle in what is known as the juvenile court laws. It is rather the surer, more constant and

State of Colorado
City and County of Denver
Juvenile Court

Summary of all Charges during the

Years __1931,shown _____ ..--,1932,shown ███████ 1933,shown ███████

Age in Years of Delinquents.

7	8	9	10	11	12	13	14	15	16	17	18

| 1 | 2 | 13 | 12 | 8 | 36 | 32 | 22 | 12 | 9 | 4 | 1 |
| | 3 | 11 | 16 | 40 | 38 | 40 | 49 | 30 | 7 | 8 | |

STATE OF COLORADO
CITY AND COUNTY OF DENVER
JUVENILE COURT

Summary of Commitments during the

YEARS—1901, shown ▬▬▬ 1902, shown ▬▬▬▬ 1903, shown ▬▬▬▬ .

	AGE IN YEARS OF DELINQUENTS.											
7	8	9	10	11	12	%	13	14	15	16	17	18

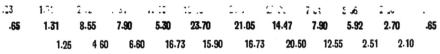

.3	1.7	2.4	.3	4.15	10.45	5.3	2.5	7.65	5.6	2.0	
.65	1.31	8.55	7.90	5.30	23.70	21.05	14.47	7.90	5.92	2.70	.65
	1.25	4 60	6.60	16.73	15.90	16.73	20.50	12.55	2.51	2.10	

intelligent application of old principles that deserves to make
noteworthy the present agitation for so-called juvenile courts.
We are infinitely more in need of men and women to do the work
than to make the laws.

ILLINOIS LAW.

The juvenile law of Illinois was the first attempt at a unifi-
cation or codification of the laws of that State relating to dependent and neglected children as well as delinquent children,
into one statute known as the juvenile law. It seems also to
have been its purpose to centralize the children's cases into one
court. It also forbade placing children under twelve years of
age in common jails or lock-ups. Statutes forbidding this, however, have existed in a great many States, including Colorado,
for twenty years. A peculiar fact is that in the various States
there has been very little effort to enforce the children's laws.
For instance, there are a number of States having on the statute books, backed by the powers of the Chancery Court in dealing with the children in its capacity of parens patriae, all the
power necessary to conduct as perfect and complete a juvenile
court as that of Colorado or Illinois, without the addition of a
word or a line of the elaborate statute known as the " juvenile
law."

COLORADO LAWS.

Colorado, before the enactment of our present juvenile law,
is an illustration of this fact. What is known as our " School
Law," approved April 12, 1899 (two months before the juvenile law of Illinois of the same year went into effect), provided that school children under sixteen, who are vicious, incorrigible, or immoral in conduct, or habitual truants from school,
or who habitually wander about the streets and public places
during school hours or in the night time, having no employment
or lawful occupation, shall be deemed juvenile disorderly persons, subject to the provisions of the Act. The act further provided that any person might file a complaint in the County Court
(now also called the Juvenile Court), and that the case could be
continued for further hearing upon the conduct of the child. This
act also provided that the School Board could appoint truant

officers who should look after the children. It will be observed therefore, that even before the Juvenile Law of Illinois of 1899 became effective, Colorado had upon her statute books every feature of the Juvenile Court of Illinois, if only availed of and put into actual practice. We have found this condition to exist in several States clamoring for Juvenile Laws. Of course we must except that feature of the law which permits us to hold legally accountable and punish parents and others for the moral delinquency of children. Colorado is at this period the first and only State in the Union which has such a law.

THE WORK AND THE LAW.

What is here said is not intended to withhold any credit from the noble men and women responsible for the embodiment of all of these features in a well-defined code, but simply to accentuate the fact that it is not so much a question of laws as a question of work *with* and for the children. It is rather a question of doing the thing. In saying this, we do not intend to discourage efforts in behalf of such a Juvenile Court system as has been finally adopted in Illinois and Colorado.

ADVANTAGES OF JUVENILE LAW.

We found it much more convenient in the handling of children's cases to embody in definite statutory form the definition of "delinquency," and "dependency," and to provide many details by statute, the working out of which without the statute would depend upon the co-operation of various officials, which might not be so easily obtained, and which would be largely voluntary.

TRUE FUNCTION OF STATE.

Another advantage of this compilation has been to emphasize and accentuate the importance of such cases and the necessity on the part of the State for greater care and more intelligent dealing in the handling of one of its greatest problems. It has resulted in a moral awakening. It has caused a revulsion against that carelessness and indifference which formerly characterized the State in its dealing with children offenders. It has, more than any other incident in the history of jurisprudence, compelled us to realize that the attitude of the State in the care and correction of the child should be as nearly parental as possible. It has also provided a better method of living up to this test. It has awakened the State to see with clearer vision that the child is not to be *reformed*, but to be *formed*; that it has every advantage while character is plastic, in the golden period of adolescence, to redeem a possible offender of the future to good citizenship before he has really become an offender at all. This should be accomplished as a wise and loving parent would accomplish it, not with leniency on the one hand or brutality on the other, but with charity, patience, interest, and what is most important of all, a firmness that commands respect, love, and obedience, and does not produce hate or ill-will. To correct the child we must often begin by correcting the parent, improving the environment in which the child lives, and adding, as far as possible, good opportunities to its life. If the parent is careless and negligent, punishment is rather for the parent than the child. If the parent is helpless, or if the environment is such as to seriously hamper the honest effort of the parent, as is often the case; or, if the natural instincts of childhood for fun, play and adventure are stifled, for instance by city ordinances, necessary for the protection of others in large cities, with the consequence of a sure violation thereof, and an unintentional disregard for the rights of others rather than viciousness or criminality, then the State simply comes to the aid of the parent and the child.

THE LAW IN DENVER AND COLORADO.

Denver is now in the fourth year of its so-called "Juvenile Court Work." Some cases were brought under the law of April 12th, 1899, but no organized effort or systematized plan was inaugurated until a year later. Up to this time there were nearly as many children proceeded against in the Justice's Court and in the Criminal Court for crime as there were in the County Court. (The County Court is also the Juvenile Court.) There was no systematized effort to bring them to one Court. There was no report system, no probation officers, no rain baths, no literature, no physical department, no relief department, none of the earnest heart to heart work and personal contact and touch with the boys, such as characterizes the present Juvenile Court work.

STATE OF COLORADO
CITY AND COUNTY OF DENVER
JUVENILE COURT

Probation Chart   All ages   Years 1902.1903.

719   44   21   23   6.12   2.92   3.20

There was no adult delinquent law. There was no juvenile improvement association, no detention school, with its wholesomeness and uplifting influence. On the contrary, there was the jail, with its filth and vermin and all its vileness, into which over two thousand Denver boys, between ten and sixteen years of age, were thrust during the six years prior to the establishment of the Juvenile Court. This meant that one out of every five mothers' sons had a taste of jail life during his formative period between 10 and 16, the most important in life, the period when examples and impressions for good or evil are most sure and lasting. One of the judges, Hon. Robt. W. Steele of the County Court, had shown the most heartfelt interest in the children's cases, and had set aside a special afternoon, generally Saturdays, for the hearing of such cases in the County Court. Some of the district judges had done the same thing. Mr. O. S. Storrs, as a member of the Board of County Visitors, and, as it has always been the case in such reforms, many of the good women of Denver, had helped to relieve the rigors and severities of the criminal law in dealing with children by their interest in such cases for several years before the Juvenile Court was established, and they are entitled to much credit for the final evolution of the system into its present condition. The Humane Society of Colorado, through its president, Hon. Walter S. Cheesman, and its efficient secretary, Mr. E. K. Whitehead, had also (as they do now) rendered much assistance in the care and protection of children, especially dependent and neglected cases.

OBJECTIONS TO JUVENILE LAW.

Whatever good results may come under any juvenile law must depend rather upon the personal, active, sincere and earnest work of those who are called upon to administer the law. Yet we would be handicapped without the law. It permits many things to be done where there is a disposition to do, which could only be accomplished with difficulty under the old law. I do not, in my own experience, know of one imaginable abuse which might be feared under the juvenile law, that could not likewise and with more probability occur under the criminal laws. The misfortune is that abuses, mistakes and failures under the criminal law, because of its very conventionality, are seldom thought of or considered; whereas the shortcomings, however inconsiderable, under the juvenile law, because it is new, are too often seized upon and held up as glaring illustrations of its failure. An official requested the Judge of the Juvenile Court to send a 15-year-old boy to jail, giving as his principal reason that, while the evidence was not conclusive, nevertheless the boy had been in jail twelve times before from the Criminal Courts, and therefore he should be sent to jail the thirteenth time. It never occurred to him that the State had failed already twelve times when he began his dire predictions that to place the boy on probation, with such aid as could be afforded him by the Court, would end in utter failure. In this particular case the boy turned out well, and after two years, is an independent and promising citizen. But suppose probation had failed? It would have had still twelve times the best of the jail. Even in England, where the criminal laws are most rigidly enforced, according to the statistics of its prison inmates, more than half of them are serving at least the second term.

Power under any law may be abused. Mistakes under any law may be made. No system is perfect. If anyone conceives the idea that the Juvenile Court was created for the purpose of correcting or reforming every disorderly child, they are, of course, mistaken. Jails and criminal courts never did that. On the contrary, criminality among the youth of this country has been amazingly on the increase. Over half of the inmates of jails, reformatories and prisons combined are under twenty-four years of age. They are there largely because of uncorrected delinquency in childhood. While the Juvenile Court and probation system will not, and cannot entirely overcome delinquency and waywardness, it will do it a great deal better than the jail and the criminal court ever did. This is the test of its success rather than the number of children it succeeds in correcting. There are failures under the juvenile law, but there were more failures under the criminal law. It must be remembered that the Juvenile Court generally deals with cases in which there has been a failure in the home, school, and often the church. These three institutions are the places through their various influences to form the character of the child. Yet when he violates the law of the land, it is the State that is called in to effect the correction. The home, of course, is the most important place of all to accomplish this. The school or the State is not to blame because it cannot always supply the deficiency of home training. Again, each home depends upon some other home, and I have known many careful and firm parents to have all of their efforts in behalf of their boys overcome by the stronger power and influence of a boy in some other home, where the rearing and training was not so good. We are the creatures more or less of all the influences and environment of our lives. The Juvenile Court is rather an aid to the home and the school in the moral training of the child. If these two latter fail, the Court, through its officers, does the best it can to supply the deficiency. It should never be resorted to until necessary, and then it needs and demands the help, assistance and co-operation of the parent and the school, and with their aid, brings to bear such additional power as it may wield in the life of a child, to correct its evil tendencies. They should realize that what is being done is in the interest of the child and, incidentally, to protect the rights of others. Of course, it is also to overcome lawlessness, secure obedience from the child and respect for the law. This is done often under difficulties, not of the Court's creating but over which it has not complete control. Understood rightly the actions of the Court will seldom merit disapproval or criticism.

THE COURT AND THE HOME.

It will be seen, therefore, that it not the province of the Juvenile Court to usurp the functions of the home. Its true province is rather to see that this function is performed as it should be. In the case of inexcusable neglect and indifference by parents, to compel them to perform this function; where there is excuse, as is frequently the case, to assist them, and finally where the parent has entirely failed or there is no home, the State must take the child and treat it as nearly as possible as the parent should.

TREATMENT OF CHILD OFFENDERS.

This Court does not tolerate the idea of the child being a criminal. It does not consider the question of punishment the important thing. If the child cannot be corrected at home, for

its own good and for the good of society at large, it is simply
sent to a State public school, where discipline is superior to that
of the home, and where it is intended to correct its waywardness
and also, in so far as it may, serve as an example to prevent
waywardness in others. The purpose is in delinquent cases, to
inspire and receive obedience, to improve and strengthen character. Force is seldom necessary. It should not be at all if
there was harmony, understanding and patience. It is only at
best a short cut to correction. It is not natural. We never release a boy upon probation until he is impressed with the idea
that he must obey. It is explained what the consequences will
be if he does not obey and keep his word. It is kindly, but
firmly impressed why all this is so, and why after all he is the one
we are most interested in and that it is *for* him we are working
and not *against* him. We want him to work *with* us and not
against us. He must, to do this, obey in the home, in the school,
and of course, he must obey the laws of the land and respect the
rights of others. We must know that he obeys. We know this
by reports from the school, signed by the teacher, every two
weeks; by reports from the neighborhood, when necessary to
investigate, and frequently, by reports from the home, and, in exceptional cases, visits to the home. And more important than
all this and above all this is the trust and confidence we impose
upon the boy himself through the administrative work of the
Court. We arouse his sense of responsibility. We understand
him as best we can and we make him understand us as best we
can.

CRIMINAL COURT AND JUVENILE COURT COMPARED.

In over 95 per cent. of cases on probation, after nearly four
years (at the writing of this report), we succeed. We do not fail
in the five per cent., for because a boy must be sent to the Industrial School is not the test of failure. It may be said that because 95 per cent. have not committed a second offence, after a
period of from one to three years, it is not the test of success.
Yet such was the test under the criminal law, and it is the only
test we have. We know that over 50 per cent. of all the boys
discharged from the courts, before the existence of the juvenile
law, were returned for further offences within the same period

upon which the estimates of results in the Juvenile Court of
Denver are here made.   As a matter of fact, from the records
investigated in the Criminal Court, over 90 per cent. were convicted of crime and over 75 per cent. of boys, under seventeen,
were sent to the jail or some State institution.   In the Denver
Juvenile Court none are convicted of crime or subjected to the
contamination of the jail, and not over five per cent. of those
first subjected to probation ever reach the Industrial School to
be cared for at the expense of the State, and (however unjust it
is) to be handicapped in life by the stigma of reform school odor.
Indeed if the number of commitments of children brought to the
Juvenile Court were as large as in the old days when they were
brought to the Criminal Court, considerably over $100,000 cash
would have been added to the burdens of the tax payers of Colorado during the past three years, for their care and maintenance.
But is this even to be thought of in connection with the saving
to the citizenship of tomorrow?

THE PRESENT COLORADO LAW AND DETAILS OF ITS OPERATION.

The first two annual reports of the Juvenile Court of Denver
represented its work under the system established in January,
1901, in which was invoked for its support the powers of the
Court as a Chancery Court, aided by the laws relating to dependent and neglected children enacted in April, 1895, and the law
relating to delinquent children, heretofore referred to, approved
April 12th, 1899.   The Court is now conducted under an elaborate set of laws prepared in November, 1902, and passed by the
Legislature of January, 1903.   With the exception of the substi-
tution of the detention school for the jail and the law holding
parents and all other citizens to a rigid legal liability for any
faults of children to which they may contribute, no other substantial changes have been made in the juvenile laws of Colorado.   The administrative work has always been of infinitely more
importance than the statutes.   The best juvenile laws in the
world without the proper people to administer them, would be
but little substantial improvement over the old criminal laws in
the correction of children.   Yet they would be preferable.

DELINQUENCY.

In defining delinquency we embodied the very broad defini-tion of that term in the Colorado School law of April 12th, 1899, and the Illinois law of 1901, adding a number of features as the result of over two years' experience, to-wit:

"The words 'delinquent child' shall include any child six-teen (16) years of age or under such age who violates any law of this State or any city or village ordinance; or who is incorrigible; or who knowingly associates with thieves, vicious or immoral persons; or who is growing up in idleness or crime; or who know-ingly visits or enters a house of ill-repute; or who knowingly pat-ronizes or visits any policy shop or place where any gaming de-vice is, or shall be operated; or who patronizes or visits any sa-loon or dram shop where intoxicating liquors are sold; or who patronizes or visits any public pool room or bucket shop; or who wanders about the streets in the night time without being on any lawful business or occupation; or who habitually wanders about any railroad yards or tracks or jumps or hooks on to any moving train, or enters any car or engine without lawful author-ity; or who habitually uses vile, obscene, vulgar, profane, or in-decent language, or is guilty of immoral conduct in any public place or about any schoolhouse. Any child committing any of the acts herein mentioned shall be deemed a juvenile delinquent person, and shall be proceeded against as such in the manner hereinafter provided. A disposition of any child under this act, or any evidence given in such cause, shall not in any civil, crim-inal or other cause or proceeding whatever in any court be law-ful or proper evidence against such child for any purpose what-ever, excepting in subsequent cases against the same child un-der this act."

We retain section 4 of the school law of April 12, 1899, with slight changes as follows:

"Sec. 4. Every child within the provisions of this act who does not attend school, as provided in section 1 of this act, or who is in attendance at any public, private or parochial school, and is vicious, INCORRIGIBLE OR IMMORAL IN CONDUCT, or who is an habitual truant from school, or who habitually wan-ders about the streets and public places during school hours with-

out any lawful occupation or employment, or who habitually
wanders about the streets in the night time, having no employment or lawful occupation, shall be deemed a juvenile disorderly
person, and be subject to the provisions of this act."

Section 1 of the School Law referred to provides as follows:

THE COMPULSORY SCHOOL LAW.

"Section 1. That in all school districts of this State, all
parents, guardians and other persons having care of children
shall instruct them, or cause them to be instructed, in reading,
writing, spelling, English grammar, geography and arithmetic.
In such districts, every parent, guardian, or other person having
charge of any child between the ages of eight (8) and sixteen
(16) years, shall send such child to a public, private or parochial
school for the entire school year during which the public schools
are in session in such districts; Provided, however, That this act
shall not apply to children over fourteen (14) years of age where
such child shall have completed the eighth grade, or may be eligible to enter any high school in such district, or where its help is
necessary for its own or its parents' support, or where for good
cause shown it would be for the best interests of such child to
be relieved from the provisions of this act; Provided, further,
That if such child is being sufficiently instructed at home by a
person qualified, such child shall not be subject to the provisions
of this act; and Provided, further, That if a reputable physician
within the district shall certify in writing that the child's bodily
or mental condition does not permit its attendance at school,
such child shall be exempt during such period of disability from
the requirements of this act. It shall be the duty of the superintendent of the school district, if there be such superintendent,
and, if not, then the county superintendent of schools, to hear
and determine all applications of children desiring for any of the
causes mentioned herein to be exempted from the provisions of
this act, and if upon such application such superintendent hearing the same shall be of the opinion that such child is for any reason entitled to be exempted as aforesaid, then such superintendent shall issue a written permit to such child, stating therein
his reasons for such exemption. An appeal may be taken from
the decision of such superintendent so passing upon such appli-

cation to the county court of the county in which such district lies, upon such child making such application and filing the same with the clerk or judge of said court within ten days after its refusal by such superintendent, for which no fee to exceed the sum of one dollar shall be charged, and the decision of the county court shall be final. An application for release from the provisions of this act shall not be renewed oftener than once in three months."

The County Courts of Colorado are declared by the Juvenile Law to be the Juvenile Courts. The law extends to the entire State. It is not limited to cities.

DEPENDENT CHILDREN.

No reference is made in the last Juvenile act to dependent or neglected children. The title of the act is "An Act Concerning Delinquent Children." We deliberately omitted dependent and neglected children from this act because: First, the law of 1895 concerning dependent children was considered sufficient for all purposes in connection with the inherent chancery and probate power of the court, under our general statute and the common law, to deal with dependent and neglected children. Second, we feared to jeopardize the constitutionality of the act by subjecting it to possible attacks on the ground that it attempted to deal with more than one subject, as our constitution forbids any one act from doing. While not admitting such objection, it was thought best not to take such chances, in view of substantial laws already existing for the present needs of our people. Third, a number of reasons because of local conditions and some legal complications peculiar to our State, not necessary to refer to, made it wise to omit dependent children from this bill. Fourth, Colorado has few dependent children, and the problem of dependency is entirely different from that presented in some of the old States containing larger cities. The delinquent child has been the class most neglected, nevertheless the present statutes relating to dependent and neglected children, while sufficient for present needs, were codified and amended into one harmonious chapter which was presented in the last Legislature, but failed of passage. It encountered no opposition but could not be reached on the calendar before the day of adjournment. It will be presented again at the next Legislature. While we consider "delinquent" and "dependent," as these terms are applied to children, more or less interchangeable, and a delinquent child simply a neglected child, it was considered the wisest policy, in view of possible objections and constitutional quibbles upon which our Supreme Court has never passed, and the addition of our parents' delinquent bill to keep the acts separate and distinct. Since this policy was adopted, however, the Supreme Court of Missouri has (within the last few months) sustained the constitutionality of the Juvenile Law of Missouri, which referred to both dependent and delinquent children, and overruled the attack made upon the law because of the embodiment of both classes in one and the same act and the limitation of the operation of the law to cities alone. Courts of other States might hold differently, however, and the matter must be controlled largely by local decisions and conditions.

PREPARATION OF LAW.

In adopting juvenile laws in other States, good lawyers, especially those versed in constitutional law, should be consulted, and a great deal will depend upon the constitution of a particular State, general statutes, the jurisdiction of courts, the fee system or the salary system of paying officials, and other details readily suggesting themselves to the lawyer, and which might be because of lack of training and experience, overlooked entirely by charity organizations, woman's clubs, civic societies, or other perfectly well meaning associations which have taken up the passage of juvenile laws. Again, with the best legal advice, difficulties may be encountered, and the law, or portions thereof, possibly upset, so that only a number of years of experience and amendment can perfect a suitable law. Those interested in this reform must not be discouraged by backsets in the court or disappointments in the administrative work by those placed in charge. A satisfactory system is bound to come in time with patient effort and no lagging of the spirit back of it.

SPECIAL FEATURES OF COLORADO LAW.

The following features are largely peculiar to the Juvenile Law of Colorado as found in its various sections.

PAID PROBATION OFFICERS are provided for, not

to exceed three, in cities of over 100,000 inhabitants, at a salary of twelve hundred dollars per year each for two of such officers, and fifteen hundred dollars per year for the chief proba- tion officer with an expense account of eleven hundred dollars a year, to be paid under the direction of the court.

HOW APPOINTED.

Provision is made for the appointment of these officers by the Judge of the court, subject, however, to the approval of the State Board of Charities and Corrections. This Board is com- posed of two women and five men, always representing our best citizenship, who are not politicians and who serve without pay. They must within thirty days after submission of the appoint- ment, reject or confirm the same. The purpose of this provision was, as far as possible, to keep politics from interfering with such appointments, and to secure a high class of service. It has worked most successfully so far. It is far superior to the volun- tary probation system of the first two years' experience of the court. There are some good reasons for and against providing for paid probation officers. In Illinois paid probation officers are not provided for, yet there are, according to reports, about 40 such officers paid in Chicago by the various charity associations, and by the city. The Mayor simply appoints a number of men as policemen and details them to the Juvenile Court, where they are appointed probation officers. They thus receive their pay as policemen and do their work as probation officers. The char- ity associations and the charitably disposed citizens are called upon to pay the salaries of quite a number of such officials, and then there are a great many who give their services without pay.

THE EXPENSE OF PROBATION.

Considering that Denver, like Chicago, has hundreds of thou- sands of dollars invested in jails, criminal courts, and hundreds of thousands to make up the salary lists of deputy sheriffs, jail- ers and policemen, and considering that over half of the crim- inals are among the young men, that at least one-fifth of all ar- rests (possibly eliminating common drunks) in the cities of this country are among the boys, it would seem a very short-sighted and inconsistent policy in providing for their protection and the prevention of crime, to refuse the expenditure of public moneys therefor, and at the same time continue to increase the appropriations into the hundreds and hundreds of thousands for the conviction and punishment of those who are criminals largely because of neglect in youth by the home and the State. The only possible advantage in favor of begging from the public to support probation officers, is the fact that it is more likely to be eliminated from politics and a better class of people employed. Yet, in principle, I think the system is wrong. It is unjust and unfair to require the charitably disposed citizen of the community to exclusively shoulder the financial burden of administering its most important laws. Some method should be devised to keep the administration of these laws out of politics, and generally a healthy public sentiment, such as exists with reference to this work in most of the cities, will do much to that end. The Judge of the Juvenile Court of Denver has never been approached by a single political leader or a single political influence in the appointment of probation officers, nor does the Judge of that Court know the politics of the probation officers.

The paid probation officers are two men and one woman, selected because of their peculiar fitness and competency for the work in hand; and, as at present constituted, each of them has had several years' experience in work either directly or indirectly related to that of the Juvenile Court. They are in the work for the love of the work rather than for the salary in it. But because one is so disposed should not be any reason why they should not be sufficiently compensated, for there is no higher class of service to the community than that of a competent and efficient probation officer. I say without hesitation that one probation officer, earnestly and enthusiastically engaged in his work, will do more in the course of a year to prevent crime than the best District Attorney can do in five years in prosecuting crime. Judge Tuley, one of the oldest and most respected members of the Circuit Court of Chicago, declared publicly that the Juvenile Court of that city had done more during its brief existence to decrease crime than all the courts of the State could do in twenty years. This is just as true as the old adage, "An ounce of prevention is better than a pound of cure."

As many voluntary probation officers may be appointed as the Court desires.

POWERS OF PROBATION OFFICER.

Paid probation officers are vested with all the power and authority of Sheriffs to make arrests and perform other duties incident to their office. In counties having a population exceeding 15,000 one probation officer may be designated by the Court by and with the consent of the Board of County Commissioners, where it is deemed necessary, upon a salary to be fixed by the Board. The purpose of this joint responsibility in appointing a probation officer is to prevent abuse under the statute, as, if left to the discretion of the County Judge in a small county, an officer might be appointed when unnecessary, as a political reward or favor. So far no complaint has been made of abuse under this section, excepting in two counties where it is claimed a paid probation officer is needed and the County Commissioners refused to permit it because of the expense.

HOW COMPLAINTS ARE FILED.

The district attorneys of the several counties in the State, as well as all probation officers appointed by the Court, are authorized to file complaints or petitions in the County Courts of the several counties of the State, declaring any child to be delinquent by briefly stating the cause of the delinquency. In the large cities like Denver the probation officers file all the petitions or complaints. We consider this better than permitting the indiscriminate filing of complaints by any citizen who has some grievance against a child, which very often does not deserve the dignity of a court proceeding. The result is that in Denver all complainants must first submit their case to the probation officers or the District Attorney. The District Attorney has properly turned all such cases over to the probation officers. It is then investigated and often settled out of court. A warning and notice to the parents by the probation officers of their responsibility to correct the child in the home is effective in a great many cases, without further action. The effect is also a distinct benefit to the entire community because of its reminding influence on all parents.

Two or three detailed monthly reports made by the probation officers are submitted in another part of this report as better indicating the detailed work of that official.

In the smaller counties of the State it is impracticable and practically impossible to have a probation officer. In nearly every county some lawyer, generally a young practitioner, acts as a Deputy District Attorney, and he files the complaints or petitions, not as prosecuting officers do in prosecuting for crime, but rather as the agent of the chancery court.

THE FEE SYSTEM OF PAYING OFFICERS.

Prosecuting officers in criminal cases are paid by the fee system in Colorado. We have heard of children being prosecuted for crime when there was no necessity for it, in order that the fees of prosecuting officers could be earned.

It was considered doubtful if the State could be deprived by statute of the right to prosecute children of sixteen years or under for crime, if it elects so to do. The danger in Colorado where the fee system exists was that prosecuting officers in some of the counties might insist upon prosecuting children for crime in order to earn the fees. It was therefore provided in the Juvenile Law, as the Legislature had an undoubted right to do, that no fees should be paid any officer in the case of a child within the provisions of the act, unless it was proceeded against under the Juvenile law, in which case a small fee is allowed, unless permission should first be given by the Juvenile Court, excepting capital cases, to prosecute for crime. The result of this provision has been to avoid the abuses feared and to secure the co-operation instead of the antagonism of the various officials of the State, when the pernicious fee system threatened all kinds of difficulties.

POWERS OF COURT NOT ABUSED.

So far there has not been a single case where any one has intimated that the rather broad powers afforded to bring children into court have been abused. Out of two thousand cases against both parents and children brought to the Juvenile Court of Denver in over three years, in only two cases have lawyers ever appeared to defend, and no exception has ever been taken to the disposition of a single case, although several hundred parents and others have been fined or sent to jail and a considerable number of children committed to institutions. Among these cases have been children and parents of very wealthy people as well as very poor people. Juvenile Courts are in operation in Pueblo, Colorado Springs, Greeley, Boulder, Cripple Creek, Leadville and several other towns, and we have yet to hear of a single charge of abuse by any Colorado court of any power under the Juvenile law.

HOW LAW EXTENDS TO ENTIRE STATE.

The law was designed primarily for the large cities where the problem of the children is very different from that of the smaller towns. It was extended, however, to the entire State, first, because it would have been of doubtful constitutionality under the constitution of Colorado to have made special laws for special cases in special towns, and, second, we believed that whatever good might be derived from the probation system might, without expense or danger of abuse, be extended to all the children of the State. The wisdom of this course has been more than apparent, as the act has been considered free from constitutional defects and legal difficulties by all of the best lawyers in the State who have examined into the question.

THE LAW IS ELASTIC AND VALID.

The Colorado law is designed to be so elastic that in case any Court ever should hold that children cannot be dealt with differently from adults with respect to their offences against the State, all of the admittedly good features of the law may be preserved and its administration in no wise seriously hampered. We have not the slightest doubt, however, that the Courts will sustain the law when called upon, upon the theory regarded by us as the proper and correct one, viz.: That the State is simply devising a method of dealing with its wards, not as criminals, but as misguided and misdirected; as those who might be criminals some day, but in childhood not yet responsible, still in the formative period, and as needing the care, help and assistance of the State rather than its punishment. The State, in other words, deals with the morals of the child, on much the same basis that it would deal with the financial welfare of a minor, who is not considered sufficiently responsible to handle his dollars or dispose of his property until he arrives at the age of twenty-one years. Surely if the State can distinguish between individuals under twenty-one in dealing with their property and money, regarding them as entitled to a different protection and a different application of rules and laws than adults, there is more reason why a different course should be pursued by the State when it comes to the question of the moral welfare of its children. The value of the future citizen to the State depends a great deal more upon how well and how carefully his morals are guarded than how wisely his money is spent.

EXCEPTIONAL CASES.

Yet we realize that there are exceptional cases of depravity and viciousness among the young, and the State retains the right, by one section of the Juvenile Law, to consider anyone of these (sixteen years or under) a proper subject for the criminal courts, and may elect, in accordance with the procedure prescribed, to prosecute such case in the criminal court, subject to all the rules and penalties of the criminal law.

CHILDREN AND PARENT CASES ALL IN ONE COURT.

Jurisdiction is by this act taken away from the police courts and justices of the peace in all cases of children offenders sixteen years of age or under, in order that such cases may be all tried in one court. Surely it is not only right but the duty of the State to legislate for the best interests of its children, and the purpose of this provision is to better enable the officers of the State to deal with the problem of delinquency, both as for the best interest of the child and for the best interest of the State. In Colorado this feature of the law is carried out to the extent of concentrating all such cases into one court. This is the County Court, declared by law to be the Juvenile Court in children's cases, having all the criminal, chancery and civil jurisdiction necessary to cases pertaining to children, parents or others effected by the juvenile laws; yet a portion of this system is rather a matter of practice and co-operation between the district attorney and the court than mandatory under the statute. Parents, citizens and others who contribute to the delinquency of children, are therefore tried in the same court before the same judge, generally on different days from the children. Fathers who fail to support their children, either physically or morally, are liable under the laws of Colorado, and in Denver are all tried in the Juvenile Court. Thus there is concentrated into one court, in one jurisdiction, under the surveillance of the same set of officials, every conceivable case involving a dependent or delinquent child, as well as those responsible for its dependency or delinquency. The school law and the child labor law are also enforced in the same court before the same judge, in Denver. Hon. H. A. Lindsley, the District Attorney for Denver, is entitled to great credit for his broad sympathy with this work, aiding, as far as it is in the power of his office to aid, the perfection of this system.

There is no reason why the same system cannot be established in other jurisdictions, and the results, as compared to those of the old methods of divided jurisdictions, different courts and different judges, will more than compensate for any effort to bring it about. We consider it a step backward rather than forward to provide for a special court limited to children's cases only unless it is given general and unlimited criminal and chancery court jurisdiction in order that it may successfully handle all cases against or concerning adults where a child is involved. In view of the doubtful constitutionality and difficulty of establishing such a court in many States, it would seem much better to confer such jurisdiction in an established and recognized court under the constitution, and if necessary provide an extra judge for such a court, fixing by practice and rule of court the time for hearing adult and juvenile delinquent cases. In the very large cities a special court may be preferable if the jurisdiction is unlimited.

DUE PROCESS OF LAW — JURY TRIAL, RIGHT TO COUNSEL, ETC.

In order to avoid constitutional difficulties or attacks upon the law, it was considered the better part of prudence to provide for trial by jury in case it is demanded; also the right to counsel, a right that could be claimed in a criminal case. In dealing with a child as a ward of the Court, for its own welfare, on the theory hereinbefore mentioned as the true one, we do not believe that any such provisions are necessary, yet their incorporation in the law was a wise precaution and may indefinitely defer, if not entirely prevent, attacks upon it. We never appoint attorneys to defend children. The Court is their defender and protector as well as corrector.

ANNUAL REPORTS FROM COURTS.

Yearly reports, containing much detailed information, to the State Board of Charities and Corrections from all the Juvenile Courts of the State are required, as furnishing interesting data of value sociologically. Names and identity of parents or children brought to the Juvenile Court are expressly prohibited by the law from being revealed in any such reports.

DETENTION SCHOOL.

The detention home or school is provided in lieu of the jail in counties of the first class (where the largest cities are located). It is mandatory upon the authorities to furnish such place, removed from any jail or lock-up. No child under fourteen years of age can be incarcerated in any jail. The detention school in Denver has proved a marked success so far, and is ably administered by Mr. and Mrs. J. P. Wright, eminently qualified by long experience as teachers and workers with boys for their position. The home is as comfortable as a family home, contains a school room, dormitory and dining room. Where it is necessary to detain children, they are kept engaged in some useful, wholesome occupation. Boys do not like to be kept in after school. They are particularly anxious not to be "kept in" in the detention school for several days or a week; and the wholesome surroundings of the place have not, as some of the pessimistically inclined would have had us believe, had the effect of encouraging rather than discouraging waywardness. It is true that many boys are returned to the detention house the second time; but it was equally true in our experience that many more were returned to the jail the second and up to the tenth and twentieth time.

JUVENILE COURT.

DETENTION HOUSE

CORRECT THE CHILD BUT PROTECT THE CHILD.

The detention school is not a cure-all. It is more effective, however, as far as there can be any effect in the correction of the child, than the jail, and from our experience a great deal more so, and at the same time, while it seeks to correct the child, it does protect the child. This the jail has never done and never can do. The jail always degrades. Admitting any shortcomings of the detention school, if there be any (and we do not pretend that it is perfect), it is hard to conceive how anyone could ask for a return to the jail, unless they belong to that class of carpers and critics who have never done anything to solve or help solve this intricate problem, but who are always ready to tear down what others have tried to build up, and who start in by assum-ing that unless a new plan is a cure-all for all delinquency, it must necessarily be a failure.

ARM OF DISCIPLINE.

The detention school is also the strong arm of discipline of the Juvenile Court. If a boy fails to report as required by the Court, it is well to have the detention school instead of the jail where he may be placed until he learns the lesson of obedience. When a boy is brought there, the superintendent ascertains his school and grade, and he is simply kept at his lessons. The su-perintendent sleeps in the same dormitory with the boys, where the beds are clean and wholesome and the surroundings pure and uplifting. The boy's environment is kept as normal and nat-ural as possible consistent with the necessities of discipline and firmness to bring about correction.

HOW BOYS ARE TRUSTED.

Many of the boys recently sent to the detention school are sent alone, with their own written orders for detention. I have likewise returned many a boy to the jail alone at all times of day and night, and never has a boy whom I sent to jail alone failed to go. With a few exceptions (generally because of utter irresponsibility) since we inaugurated the system, all boys who have been sent to the Industrial School have been sent alone, and not one out of the eighteen thus dealt with so far has failed to go without any officer or anyone at the school knowing he was coming; yet this involves a trip through a crowded city, a change of cars in the railroad yards, speeding across the plains into the foothills, and landing a half mile from the Industrial School gate. This feature will be referred to more in detail under the chapter on "Administrative Work."

COMMITMENTS AND INSTITUTIONS.

With few exceptions the commitments in delinquent cases thus far made by the Juvenile Court have been made to the Industrial School for boys at Golden, and for girls at Morrison. These are educational institutions maintained by the State and declared by law to be educational and not penal. Our laws forbid the State to pay any private institution for the care of its wards. It provides ample facilities in its own schools, conducted by State officials, for the care of both delinquent and dependent children. Children may be sent to private institutions approved by the State Board of Charities and Corrections, but the expense thereof must be provided for by the institution itself, or from some private source.

RELIGIOUS INSTRUCTION.

All denominations may conduct religious instructions in the State schools or homes.

ADOPTED INTO HOMES.

About half of the dependent children brought to the Court have been adopted into homes at once. All others are sent to the State Home for Dependent Children near Denver, where homes are found as rapidly as possible. There are State agents representing the institution who keep track of the child to be assisted to see that his home is suitable and treatment proper.

STATE OF COLORADO
CITY AND COUNTY OF DENVER
JUVENILE COURT

Parent's Chart.

Parents brought before the Court and

fined for contributing to delinquency

of Children —   № 197.

2.

Persons other than Parents —   № 40.

————— 3. —————

Parents if others committed to jail on above charge. № 40.

ADULT DELINQUENT CHART SHOWING PARENTS BROUGHT TO COURT;
ALSO CITIZENS OTHER THAN PARENTS, IN 1903.

CONSTRUCTION OF LAW.

Our delinquent act provides that it "shall be liberally construed in order that the care, custody and discipline of the child shall approximate as nearly as may be that which should be given by his parents, and that, as far as practicable, any delinquent child shall be treated, not as a criminal, but as misdirected and misguided, and needing aid, encouragement and assistance." In the Juvenile Court of Denver we follow out the letter and spirit of this law under what we term the administrative work of the Court, which must depend largely upon the particular judge and officials administering the law as well as the jurisdiction, particular class of city, and the character of the problems it is called upon to face, varying as they do with different localities and populations. The administrative work of each Court, therefore, must depend largely upon a great many things, and what could be done in one jurisdiction might be very impracticable in another. What has been done in Denver in accordance with this direction of the statute, will be more particularly discussed under the head of "Administrative Work."

ADULT DELINQUENCY LAW--PARENTS AND OTHERS RESPONSIBLE.

The most important feature of our children's law is, "An act to provide for the punishment of persons responsible for or contributing to the delinquency of children."

"Section 1. In all cases where any child shall be a delinquent child or a juvenile delinquent person, as defined by the statute of this state, the parent or parents, legal guardian, or person having the custody of such child, or àny other person, responsible for, or by any act encouraging, causing or contributing to the delinquency of such child, shall be guilty of a misdemeanor, and upon trial and conviction thereof shall be fined in a sum not to exceed one thousand dollars ($1,000), or imprisoned in the county jail for a period not exceeding one (1) year, or by both such fine and imprisonment. The court may impose conditions upon any person found guilty under this act, and so long as such person shall comply therewith to the satisfaction of the court the sentence imposed may be suspended."

SOME INTERESTING CASES IN POINT.

Now, how does this work? A few illustrations will suffice.

ON THE TRACKS AND STEALING COAL.

Here are three boys brought in for stealing coal from the railroad company, or wandering about the tracks. Either of these things are declared by the children's delinquency act to constitute the child a delinquent. Now, this law was not intended for the benefit of the railroad companies unless that benefit shall be coincident with that of the children, which is probably true. Wandering on the railroad track may result in the loss of life or limb. It may cost the company a damage suit. Among the poor classes (and ninety per cent. of the boys who do this thing are so unfortunately situated) boys take coal from the cars. Some boys are encouraged in it by their parents; others do it because they see such boys doing it. The example is contagious. They will run from the officer if they see him coming. They know they are doing wrong. The next step is stealing brasses or appliances about the cars, which I have known to cause serious damage to the railroads and jeopardy to life and limb of the citizens; or the boys are breaking in cars, stealing fruit and other things, and the first thing we know, we have a completely developed thief as years progress and conscience and moral sensibility are hardened, and so the boy is in the end hurt worst of all. Now, where did this trouble begin? It began in the failure of the parents to do their duty towards the child; so, before the boy has reached the brass stealing stage, the burglary stage, or has been maimed or injured, he is brought to court, perhaps for the mere fact of being on the tracks. He is told kindly but firmly the very things here set out. His parents are brought with him and they are told the same thing, and they find for the first time that they may have to pay out money or stay in jail for letting the boy go on the tracks. Such parents are generally poor and by the terms of the act we impose conditions in the sentence against them. For instance, we may say to a delinquent father: "Mr. Jones, we will fine you $25.00 and costs. We will require you to pay $5.00 of that fine, and suspend the balance on condition that you keep that boy off the railroad and in the school. You can do it if you look after him and take more interest in him and know where he is. If you do not, you will pay the balance of this fine or go to jail." Perhaps we may suspend the entire penalty, so long as the child fails to return to the tracks. In some cases a jail sentence of thirty days has been imposed and three days enforced and twenty-seven suspended on condition the offence is not repeated. This has a wholesome effect on an entire neighborhood. Not to exceed two out of one hundred children of parents thus dealt with have so far been returned to court.

CARELESS PARENTS.

It is really astonishing how little care and attention is given by many parents to their children. It is troublesome and tiresome very often for them to do their duty. This law awakens them to a realizing sense of their responsibility to the child and if not done voluntarily that it can be enforced by the statute in a most salutary manner. If you will read the section defining delinquency you will observe that there is hardly any kind of an offence that a child can commit that the parent or others cannot be held responsible for.

SENDING CHILDREN TO EVIL PLACES.

Supposing a man sends a boy to the saloon; whether it be the manager of the messenger company, a citizen or parent, the individual that did that thing, as well as the barkeeper or the saloonkeeper who let the child have the liquor, has contributed to the delinquency of that child. The child was a delinquent by the terms of section 1 of the delinquent act when it visited or entered the saloon; it would neither have visited nor entered the place if the man or woman had not sent it there. Now, is this not just, and is it not doing more than ever to reach the root of the problem?

A TWELVE-YEAR-OLD THIEF.

I know a twelve-year-old boy who (by the criminal law) is a thief. His precocity in this direction is amazing. I studied the history of his little life and here was the beginning. A man sent him with a note to the saloon. He went to the saloon as a messenger, still innocent of the taste of liquor, and, up to that time, of any theft beyond apples from the corner grocery. The note directed that he take the liquor to a house of prostitution. In that house the boy received his first drink. Two months afterwards he began to "knock down;" that is, overcharge when he could for amounts collected on messages and to scheme in other directions to get money to buy liquor. Now, I suppose that the messenger company would have wanted to arrest the boy and send him to the Reform School for taking its money. Did you ever stop to think of the inequality of justice (or injustice) in such a result? Yet I have known it to be actually done time and time again. Of course, that boy may have been a thief, but the chances are he would not have been if the men and women involved had done their duty towards the child. The men and women involved are brought in in Colorado and heavily fined or jailed, or possibly placed on probation. Yet under the law now existing in other States they go "scot free" and the child is stigmatized with theft, or burglary, and on the threshold of its little life branded as a criminal. You will see how the whole spirit of this law is to prevent this kind of injustice and why the law is for the child. Here is an actual case: Little Henry stole a bicycle; he wanted to get money to buy liquor. Little Henry's mother had sent him to the saloon to get liquor for herself, never thinking about the child. Now, little Henry chums with little Joe. Joe's mother never sent him to the saloon, but conducted a quiet Christian home; yet Joe was a boy, with a boy's natural instincts to follow a leader, controlled by the "gang," loyal to his chum, thoughtless and easily misguided and misdirected, moral character still undeveloped Now, then, little Henry's mother not only made her own boy a thief (of course, without realizing it), but also made another mother's boy (who never did what she did) just as big a thief. Now, under the law of Colorado, we deal with firmness and yet look with kindness and consideration upon poor little Henry, ten years old, but we brought in his mother, the saloon-keeper and the bar-keeper for contributing to his delinquency. Making them respect it and do their duty helps us to correct the child. We remove the causes as far as we can.

Here are four or five boys running on the street at night, bumming around cheap theaters. They are, by the definition in section 1 of the act, delinquent. Their parents may be brought in for contributing thereto, for they will have a hard time to show that had they done their duty to their children they would not have been at home in bed. We have now two men charged with contributing to the delinquency of four young Dick Turpins, 11 and 12 years of age, by selling each of them dangerous fire-arms for money they had stolen from a drunken man whom they had steered into an alley back of the saloon and robbed. The youngest, a handsome boy of 11 (but inured to the slums and living as in an atmosphere of vileness), who engineered the scheme, said to me: "Judge, if Mr. Blank can sell the kids whiskey on Sunday when you say it is against the law, and the cop don't care, why can't we swipe things?" Such is the power of a bad example. The law would as far as possible compel men and women to set good examples.

A CHECK ON BOY BUMS.

Here is the brakeman or the conductor on the railroad who assists boy tramps to move from place to place and does not materially prevent them from "hooking" on the cars. I have known some men to encourage this sort of thing. They may be brought in for contributing to the delinquency of such a child, and so it goes. The general managers of all the railroads of Colorado have notified their trainmen of this law by circular letter, so that boy bumming is more difficult than ever. The law is very elastic, and success, of course, depends upon its wise, intelligent, tactful and firm administration.

PROBATION OF MEN AND WOMEN FOR FAULTS OF THE CHILD.

It is true we have sent men to jail for selling cigarettes or liquor to boys under this law. We have imposed heavy fines upon a great many men, but in many such cases we have placed the parents and the citizens upon probation, as well as the children. They have reported and, in doing so, have become the friends and co-workers of the Court. Some of the best friends we have, who have helped us most to stop the selling of liquor to boys in certain neighborhoods, have been saloon-keepers and bar-keepers who had originally violated the law, but who had

really never stopped to think what they were doing and did not
really intend to harm the child.   There are big-hearted men in
this class, and more success can sometimes be gained, in proper
cases, by getting them to fight with you instead of against you.
I know an intelligent liquor dealer who told me in open court that
he never realized how crime commenced and how it spread, and
what his responsibility was for the boy whom he wanted to arrest for stealing; that he had his first lesson in the Juvenile
Court and he stood ready to help punish any man who would
sell a child liquor.

THE MESSENGER COMPANY AND THE BOYS.

After the enactment of the Adult Delinquent Law, we notified the various telegraph and messenger companies that boys
under 16 on duty, going to saloons, gambling houses and other
evil resorts (the mere visiting or entering of which placed them
in the class known as delinquents) would be prosecuted.   The
managers of the Western Union, the Postal and the A. D. T., with
their counsel, held a consultation with the Judge of the Juvenile
Court after the law became effective, and agreed to obey it in
letter and spirit, and promised that, for the evening and night
service, no boy under 16 should be employed, and that boys under
16 upon day service would not be called upon to answer calls
to any of the places mentioned. So far they have obeyed the law.

THE EVILS OF STREET EMPLOYMENT--THE POWER OF EXAMPLE.

We have found, after a careful study of child crime, that
the power of example is a most potent factor. For instance, more
than half of all city school boys are addicted to swearing. Why?
Because, in the streets, even if not in the home, they constantly
hear men swear. You send them to Sunday school and they learn
they are violating one of the commandments they are taught to
obey. But men pay no attention to it; then why boys? Boys are
imitative. They want to do what men do. The constant violation
of one certainly does not help the observation of the other commandments. I have had many boys around my table in my
chambers upon many an evening, being very much a boy myself,
and learning all they know, talking with them just as one boy

would talk with another; living in their world, in their very atmosphere, and then I have been greatly helped to trace the various causes which seemed to account for weaknesses and waywardness. I believe a most fruitful cause is that of the messenger service in cities. Boys are sent to places where they see men
violating the laws, engaged in immorality, and they soon become
calloused and indifferent, their conscience ceases to respond to
nobler things, and because men do these things, why not boys?
The fact that the boy sees men or women engaged in those things
which we would caution him against makes it more difficult to
bring him through the period of adolescence to a clean, decent
and wholesome manhood. I am perfectly aware that some of our
best men have gone through the fire of these things in boyhood,
but they are the exception rather than the rule. They have
become good men, not because of such environment, but in spite
of it—because in their lives the good overcame the evil. Thousands of these children, not so fortunate, go down to destruction
every year in the cities of this nation. I know that most messenger boys, as well as newsboys, in cities, especially, are, compared to what their child life should be, and what any decent parent would want it to be, impure and unclean. I have listened to
their talk in the alleys and about the newspaper offices. They
have confided to me the very worst side of their lives and I
know whereof I speak. It is no discredit to the boys. The discredit is to those who are responsible for them during the sacred
period of adolescence. Their weakness, if it be such, is rather
misfortune than crime. No responsible father or mother would
want their boy or girl brought up in a home where there is swearing, drinking, licentiousness, deception and fraud all around
them, yet this is the environment and the life into which thousands of our city boys are thrust every year, largely because of
their work in the streets. The best way to improve a boy is to
improve his environment and add to his opportunity for good,
and, so far as laws can accomplish this end, they should be devised and enforced.

COMPULSORY EDUCATION AND HOW THE SCHOOLS HELP.

There is no more important adjunct to the Juvenile Court of
Denver than the compulsory school law and the aid rendered

the court by the school officials. Colorado has one of the best compulsory education systems in the Union. The law, as it at present stands, is the joint result of the teachers' association and the Juvenile Court of Denver. It was fathered by the County Judges' Association of Colorado as being necessary to a perfect Juvenile Court system in this State, and without it, the child labor law and the assistance of the schools in its enforcement, the efficiency and system which now exists in the handling of the delinquent child problem in Denver could not well be maintained. A few defects still exist in the compulsory education law which we sought to correct in the last Legislature, and, having failed, will probably be able to straighten out at the next session. They do not, however, affect the work in Denver. They relate more particularly to the smaller school districts in which school attendance officers are not provided. Sections 1 and 4 of our school law have already been set forth herein. The following salutary features may be noted:

SPECIAL FEATURES OF SCHOOL LAW.

The common grammar school education (from the first to the eighth grade) is made compulsory as far as possible for all children between 8 and 16 years of age, in some public, private or parochial school.

The law applies to the entire State and not to particular districts. A child must attend school during the entire school year and not for limited periods, as in many school laws.

EXEMPTIONS.

The law is made elastic by the following exemptions: All children who have completed the eighth grade or are eligible to enter a high school in their district.

If over 14 years of age, where the child's help is necessary for its own or parents' support.

Where, for good cause, it would be for the best interest of the child to be relieved from the provisions of the act or where it is being sufficiently instructed at home by persons qualified, or where a reputable physician in the district shall certify in writing that the child's bodily or mental condition does not permit of his attendance at school, he may be exempt during such period of disability.

The authority to pass upon such cases for exemption is vested in the superintendent of schools of the various districts, and, where there is no superintendent of the district, in the county superintendent of schools. The hearing may be had before this officer upon application for exemption; an appeal may be had to the Juvenile Court in which the district is situated without expense to the child or parent to exceed the sum of $1 for the filing and entering of papers and orders.

SCHOOL ATTENDANCE OFFICERS.

Paid school attendance officers are provided for. Denver has three, of whom Mr. John J. Smith is the pioneer, and an officer of exceptional ability, having rendered efficient service to the schools of the city during the four years of his incumbency.

Truancy is regarded simply as delinquency and may be dealt with either under the Juvenile law or the school law. The law is enforced in the Juvenile Court both as to children and parents. Parents may be fined a thousand dollars and sent to jail for a year for inexcusable failure to keep their children in school. As a rule small fines and sentences are sufficient.

PARENTAL SCHOOL.

Four years ago the Legislature provided that the school board in Denver should build and maintain a parental school; that no child who had committed an offense against other laws of the State should be confined therein. The law limited this institution to the care of truant children. As a result of the probation system afterwards established, and the bringing in of parents and compelling them to shoulder the responsibility, truancy has been reduced to a minimum in Denver, and the officers of the Juvenile Court are all of the opinion that there is not at present sufficient occasion for the expense and maintenance of a parental school. The motives of the good people responsible for the parental school bill are not to be questioned. Their thoughtfulness was a little premature, but may bear fruit in time. I think it is well to let the law remain upon the statute books, as the time may come, as the city grows, when we may need the parental school, as it is no doubt needed in Chicago and some other larger cities. When the parental school bill was passed, the Juvenile Court and probation system as now existing had not been devised, nor was it in contemplation, and, without it, we should no doubt have needed the parental school as those who fostered it insisted, and as to which they were entirely right at that time, and under the conditions as they then existed. We believe it to be more economical and in accordance with sound principles to continue to hold parents responsible for the truancy of their children and place the habitual truants upon probation. When this method fails, we generally find that the habitual truant is also an habitual thief (as defined by the criminal law), so that he could not be sent to the parental school under the terms of the law as it now stands. Money spent to improve the probation system and detention home is more practical and economical at the present time.

The Industrial School for Boys at Golden, however, under its present efficient management, differs very little from a parental school.

SCHOOL LAW ENFORCEMENT.

Truancy leads to a dangerous form of idleness, deception and disobedience in child life and is, therefore, one of the chief causes of crime. We believe that the wisest economy that can be practiced by the school board for the benefit of the State is to rigidly enforce the compulsory school law. The Juvenile Court is under lasting obligations to Prof. Aaron Gove, superintendent of education, and Prof. C. E. Chadsey, his able assistant, upon whom was placed the important responsibility of administering that part of the school law incumbent upon the school board. A mere casual study of the relation of truancy to child crime, and, of course, criminality in general, should convince the school board that the superintendent of compulsory education is one of the most important officials they have to appoint. The enforcement, not only of the compulsory school law, but of the child labor law of Colorado, in Denver devolves largely upon him. The great tact, judgment and discretion of Superintendent Chadsey in the first year of this important work under the new laws is worthy of especial commendation and can not be too highly appreciated by the people of Denver. Our laws have been made elastic to a certain extent in order to avoid abuses which might grow up under either a too rigid or too lax system of compulsory education and child labor laws. The success of such legislation depends upon both of these features.

CHILD LABOR LAW.

A child labor law too stringent in its provisions so as to lead to absurdities and force children into idleness and therefore into crime, may become as dangerous as a lax law or no law at all upon this subject, because if impractical and severe in its terms, admitting of no exceptions or no discretion wisely vested in competent authorities, it might fall into disuse and disrespect and fail of enforcement and thus become practically a dead letter. Upon Prof. Chadsey has also largely fallen the working out of the enforcement of that part of the law devolving upon the schools. It has been done through active and earnest co-operation between the schools and the Juvenile Court where the enforcement of this trinity of laws, namely, the juvenile law proper, the compulsory education law, and the child labor law, is centered in Denver. It has been a tremendous undertaking, fraught with difficulties that the uninitiated can hardly appreciate. We can not expect to achieve perfection or even an entirely satisfactory condition within a year. It is going to take several years of work and experience to put that system for which we are planning and working into that state of perfection which will equally satisfy both school authorities and the Juvenile Court. Patience and charity for any shortcomings on the part of either is more than earned and justified.

ENFORCEMENT OF CHILD LABOR LAW.

The three paid school attendance officers in Denver are the inspectors (by the terms of the school law) of all stores, factories, etc., as to compliance with the law. Officers of the Humane Society are also inspectors. With the assistance of the Humane Society and the district attorney, a number of convictions have been had in the Juvenile Court for the violation of the child labor laws and the extreme penalty permitted by the law has been imposed in every case. The present conditions in Denver respecting child labor have been approved by a committee appointed by the Woman's Club, who have thoroughly investigater the matter, and reported it as being as satisfactory as could be expected. It is far in advance of what it used to be in the old days.

CHILD LABOR AND COMPULSORY EDUCATION.

The child labor law of Colorado vests a discretionary power in the judge of the Juvenile Court in cases of children between fourteen and sixteen years of age as to whether their occupation and the hours thereof are dangerous to health. No child labor law can be as effective as it should be unless supplemented by a compulsory school law. The compulsory school law of Colorado is really as effective to prevent improper child labor as the child labor law proper. Under its provisions (unless within some exemption) the child under 16 years of age must finish the eighth grade (the highest) of the grammar school (or the parochial school where the grades correspond to those of the public school), and it is very seldom that that class of children for whose protection the child labor laws were enacted have finished the eighth grade. The schools of Colorado are in session from the 1st of September to about the middle of June of each year, and in nearly every part of the State. Section 4 of the child labor law of Colorado is as follows:

"Sec. 4. Any person who shall take, receive, hire or employ any child under the age of fourteen years in any underground work or mine, or in any smelter, mill or factory, shall be guilty of a misdemeanor, and upon conviction thereof shall be fined not less than fifty dollars, nor more than five hundred dollars, and shall be imprisoned in the county jail not less than thirty days, nor more than three months."

Section 1 of the same act provides that "no child sixteen years of age or less shall labor or work in any mill, factory, manufacturing establishment, shop or store, or in or about coal or other mines, or any other occupation not herein enumerated which may be deemed unhealthful or dangerous, for a greater number than eight hours in the twenty-four day, except in cases where life or property is in imminent danger, or in the week before and following Christmas day. Provided, That any child between the age of fourteen and sixteen years coming within the provisions of this act may be exempted from the provisions thereof, if, in the opinion of the judge of the County Court (which is the Juvenile Court) of the county in which said child resides, it would be for for its best interests to be so exempted. Application may be made in writing to any county judge (Juvenile Court) by any such child, its parent or guardian, to be granted such exemption, when it shall be the duty of such judge to hear the same and inquire particularly into the nature of the employment sought. No fees shall be charged or collected in any such case."

"Sec. 2. All paper mills, cotton mills and factories where wearing apparel for men or women is made, ore reduction mills or smelters, factories, shops of all kinds and stores, may be held to be unhealthful and dangerous occupations within the meaning of this act at the discretion of the court."

The penalty for the violation of this section of the act by employers is a fine of not less than $100 nor more than $500 or imprisonment in the county jail for not less than two nor more more than four months, or by both such fine and imprisonment in the discretion of the court, for each offense.

IMPRACTICABLE FEATURES OF CHILD LABOR LAW REMEDIED.

The Juvenile Court was permitted to add an amendment to the present child labor law, which, in the opinion of the writer, saved it from defeat and gave us the present act in its rather unsatisfactory form. It is much better than the old law, where the age limit was twelve and the extent of the penalty was fifty dollars fine. The somewhat impractical feature of the law in forbidding children sixteen years of age or under from working more than eight hours in a store or any possible occupation, has been eliminated by the discretion that now vests in the Juvenile Court to exempt those between fourteen and sixteen from its operation where it would appear to be for the best interest of the child. But for this amendment we feared the act would have been in many cases impracticable and might have thrust boys and girls into idleness and crime if there had been a serious attempt to enforce it. In fact, the Governor would have probably vetoed the law if left in its original shape. There are a great many stores, shops and offices in which it will not injure children between fourteen and sixteen years of age to work nine hours, the usual time for such industries to be open in Denver. The law should be amended to make more certain the penalties provided, as it now contains two rather inconsistent provisions, one of which was forced in the bill contrary to the wish of those interested in it.

WORK AND PLAY.

I firmly believe in play and happiness in childhood, and yet I fear at the present time there may be more occasion in Denver for alarm at the failure of boys, in particular between fourteen and sixteen years of age, to do any kind of useful work than there is at the danger of their being overworked. After all, in such cases, it is not so much a question of work as the kind of work and the time employed. One of the greatest difficulties with Denver boys, and I think with boys generally, is idleness. If not employed at some useful thing they are generally on the streets or in the alleys, the downtown public pool rooms and bowling alleys, engaged not always in wholesome play, but too often in the most demoralizing character of dawdling, idling, cigarette smoking and dirty story telling, with absolutely no thought of work or the serious side of life. They are too constantly occupied with thoughts of "having a good time" and some rather perverted notions of what a good time is. Too many of our boys thus reach the age of moral and legal responsibility without the slightest conception of work. They are too often more concerned as to how much they earn than as to how well they do their work. This is one of the features of work with boys and will be spoken of more at length under the head of "Administrative Work" of the Juvenile Court.

WISDOM OF CHILD LABOR LAWS.

We must not be understood as depreciating the importance of wise child labor laws and their rigid enforcement for the protection of the children of the Union, but in enforcing this protection we must be careful lest we overlook the importance of work, the right kind of work, and a certain amount of work, especially good impressions as to the importance of work and the exaction of a certain amount of work as one of the most important preventatives of delinquency.

On the other hand, it must be said that most boys will work if given any kind of an encouraging opportunity. The lack of this chance is more responsible for idleness than any disposition that way. Ninety-six per cent. of our boys are forced out of school into life in the grammar grades. They must have a chance to earn a living or become idlers and loafers, sure beginnings of crime. Their education too often has not equipped them for earning more than the most scant wages. An opportunity between the sixth and eighth grades in our city schools for the children of the toiling masses to learn some kind of useful trade or valuable work with the hands would do more to prevent delinquency than any other one thing, in my judgment. A boy of thirteen to sixteen might then go to the plumber, gasfitter, or carpenter, at a decent wage, instead of to the messenger service and the street.

SUMMARY OF LAWS.

It will be seen from the preceding that by the Juvenile Court system of Colorado is meant a number of things, to-wit:

First—The act concerning delinquent children.

Second—The act concerning dependent children.

Third—The act holding parents and others responsible for the moral delinquency of children.

Fourth—The act holding fathers legally responsible for the physical support, care and maintenance of children.

Fifth—The compulsory education law.

Sixth—The child labor law.

Seventh—The various statutes providing for the punishment of cruelty to children.

Eighth—That co-operation betwen officials whereby all of these laws for the protection of the children of the State are enforced in one Court having a complete and unlimited jurisdiction to deal with every aspect of the situation before one Judge, with a set of earnest and efficient paid officers for the enforcement of the laws. This Court is called the Juvenile Court.

Ninth—The active, persistent and earnest enforcement of these laws.

Tenth—The administrative work of the Court, the work with the boys and girls as well as for them and their work and co-operation with the Court.

The full text of all these laws may be had from the Secretary of State, at Denver, Colorado.

CHAPTER III

The Administrative Work

ADMINISTRATIVE WORK.

Of more importance than the law is the administrative work, and under this title we shall deal with what is at the same time the most interesting features of the Juvenile Court.

First in what we have termed the "*Report System*" has, at the writing of this report, been in force for nearly four years. The boys brought to the Juvenile Court of Denver, as will be seen from the chapter relating to our laws, must necessarily belong to one of two classes—school boys or working boys. Three-fourths of the boys in our Court are school boys.

TWO CLASSES OF BOYS.

Idling about the streets during school hours for boys sixteen years of age, or under, is expressly prohibited by law. If, therefore, the boy is not in school he must be at work. Of course, there are exceptional cases where a boy with good excuse is unable to get work or for some exception in the law is out of school. When a boy is brought to the Juvenile Court we ascertain his age, school, grade, teacher, neighborhood, and a few salient facts regarding his home and parentage. If for any reason exempted from school attendance, he is classed as a working boy, and we immediately concern ourselves regarding his employment, the character thereof, the number of hours, etc. If he has no employment we make every effort to assist him to get employment.

GIRLS.

What is said about boys in this report applies generally to girls, but as there is not more than one girl to ten boys to be dealt with by the Juvenile Court we speak in this report rather of the boys. This must not convey the impression that the girls are neglected. Their cases are given the same careful attention, but in many respects present a more difficult problem than the boys.

Idleness is not tolerated if there is any reasonable way to prevent it. The "school boy," if a delinquent, is kindly but firmly impressed with his duty to obey the law, to respect authority and obey first in the home and then in the school, with the assurance that there will be no likelihood then of his violating the law of the land. He is impressed with the idea that he must overcome evil with good and make up for his delinquency by being just as decent and good as he can in the home, the neighborhood and the school.

WHY WE GET REPORTS.

Now how are we to know of results? First, by our placing implicit confidence and trust in the boy (I shall speak of this more at length hereafter); second, by his giving some evidence of being worthy of this trust and confidence. We impress him with the idea that we have no doubt whatever that he will keep his word, that he will respect his honor and the confidence we put in him, and that no one will question his doing it, and that we may have a record of that fact, we ask the boy himself voluntarily to get a report from his teacher every other Friday preceding the session of the Juvenile Court every other Saturday. This report is made upon a printed card, and details conduct in school and school attendance. It is graded: excellent, good, fair and poor. It is soon understood that "good" is satisfactory, "fair" is passable, "excellent" is particularly pleasing to us, and "poor" is very displeasing. Any boy that brings a poor report at the morning session is made to understand that it is "not square." Very few people understand how the report system of the Denver Juvenile Court is operated, and I have never yet known of an individual who came to observe it who did not go away enthusiastic over the plan, though I have known some who had objections and criticism before witnessing its operation at the morning session. But after attending the court, these have been the most outspoken in commending it. It has the commendation of the school superintendents, school principals and teachers of Denver. Of course there are some defects, and sometimes some mistakes and failures.

REPORT SYSTEM DESCRIBED.

Now let us get an idea of the report system in operation. The number of boys reporting varies all the way from 100 to 200 during the school year. Every alternate Saturday during the school year, we have what is known as "Juvenile Court Day." This does not mean that it is the only day upon which Juvenile cases are tried. On the contrary, there is hardly a day in the week when I come from the bench at five·o'clock after a busy day's session of the Civil Court, which grinds almost continuously and is occupied generally with common law cases, that we do not have a "five-o'clock docket," which means some child's case. These cases are heard in Chambers around my table and a great deal of time given to each, the probation officer being present with his reports, also the parents and only those interested. On the particular Saturday mornings of regular "Juvenile Court Day" only a few cases may be tried, yet a visitor would find assembled an average throughout the year of 150 school boys. At least 80 per cent. of these boys are mere average school boys, no different from other boys; they have simply been caught in some violation of the law which was of a sufficiently serious character to be brought to the attention of the court for correction. Probably half of all delinquent cases are what we classify as mischievous cases. Not to exceed 25 per cent. require extraordinary care and attention, or visitation of the homes by probation officers, or frequent special reports to the Judge in Chambers. They have been classified as nearly as possible into two divisions:

"AVERAGE BOYS" and "DIFFICULT BOYS."

The character of offense is also classified, as explained elsewhere herein. No girls are present. The girls have reported on the previous Friday afternoon. There are generally comparatively few girls whom it is considered necessary to have report. They have been taken in hand by the lady probation officer and talked to kindly and interestingly regarding their work in school. Quite frequently the Judge also talks with these girls. None of these girls thus reporting have been guilty of anything involving their morality. Such cases are generally differently cared for. In the Court Room, upon this Saturday morning, counsel tables· have been removed, chairs have been placed in the long court room, and it has the appearance of a school room as far as possible. The probation officers are at the table provided in front of the boys. The Judge does not occupy the bench. He comes down among the boys at the table immediately in front of them.

SATURDAY MORNING TALKS.

At the opening of court I generally proceed to deliver a short "Saturday morning talk." It is made as spicy and interesting as possible. No effort is made to preach to the boys. I talk to them very much as if I were one of them discussing some ordinary boy's troubles, in illustrating a point or inculcating a principle. Their duties as little citizens are impressed upon them. They are often told that they are among the best boys in Denver. For the few exceptions, we have the greatest pity and sorrow. Some of them have done things in the past that they despise as much as we do; they know that we do not despise the boys; they should not be afraid to be caught as most boys are. They should be afraid to do wrong because it hurts them more than it does anyone else. We do not pity so much the man who loses his property or has been the victim of his act as we do the boy who committed the act. He is the subject of our commiseration. (After a wordy war with a certain Captain of Police once over what to do with five boys who stole five bicycles, I discovered the trouble arose over the difference between us. He was trying to redeem the bicycles. We were trying to redeem the boys. I told him that five American boys were worth more to the State of Colorado than the bicycles. He finally agreed with me. I had my way, and all the boys are today doing well and are promising citizens.) So we are there to help them, not to hurt them; to prove to the world that they are good boys, not bad boys. They must help us prove our faith. We can help, but we cannot carry. It is impossible for them to be bad unless they will it so and we know they are not that kind. Often I am compelled to tell them with sorrow rather than with anger, of some boy too weak to do right, to keep his word, to be square, and with a hope that I may strengthen him to be square and to be strong, and because I love him and not because I hate him or am angry at him, I must send him to the industrial school. I do this also because the law says I must do it. If a boy can not be strong enough at home to respect the rights of others, and obey, we have to send him where he will learn the lesson. And then I will put it to the boys, if So and So has been "square" in doing a certain thing, and if he is not an object of pity and his act an object of contempt, and, of, course, there is a unison of affirmative opinion. And in some of the "gangs" of boys I have known them to absolutely outlaw a boy who went back upon his word and repeated an offense for which all of the members of a gang have been brought to the Juvenile Court. One case I have in mind was that of forty boys, every one of whom had come voluntarily to me and admitted their misdemeanors under the direction, largely, of four or five boys who had been caught. Only one of them ever committed a second offense, and it was of a different character. I remember some of these boys were in my Chambers one afternoon when this particular boy came in, and they absolutely ignored him. This happened over a year ago. It was only recently that this one boy, out of the entire crowd, who had repeated a serious offense, brought me a splendid letter from his teacher, saying that he was one of the best boys in school, in addition to which the boy told me "on the square" that he had never been guilty of any other offense, and he wanted me to "square him" with the rest of the boys, which of course I shall be glad to do.

SUBJECTS OF THE "TALKS."

These Saturday morning talks are generally upon some subject that is close to a boy's heart and respecting his own world, the discussion of which keeps him in his own atmosphere, as it were, and does not try to lift him to a plane where he is not at home. For instance, a tattle-tale is called by every Denver boy, a "snitch." Every boy knows that if he tells on one of his companions he is outlawed. I think teachers often make a great mistake in compelling boys to tell on each other without considering the penalty to which the boy subjects himself in the world of "Boyville." It also very often tends to make a boy a little sneak and gets him the reputation of being a "knocker," or a "sissy boy." There may be times when it is necessary and proper to compel a boy to tell upon another. If so, it should be done in a way that will protect the boy.

The subject of the Saturday morning talk may be, "Snitching:" When to "snitch" and when not to "snitch." The boys are immediately interested. It is a common topic in Boyville. You have no trouble in getting their attention. There is no scraping of feet, uneasiness, and sliding about in the chairs, anxious to get out. They will listen long if you will only stay and talk to them. Under this title the boys learn, possibly for the first time, the duties of individuals towards each other and the State as citizens. For instance, that if one citizen saw another going into a store to steal, and knew he was going to steal, and made no effort to prevent it, he might be an accessory before the fact and as guilty as the man who stole. If, after the theft it was learned that a second party had participated in the enjoyment of the ill-gotten gains, he would be an accessory after the fact, unless he informed upon the man. The result is that they all agree that in the particular crowd they belong to they will do all they can to keep other boys from doing improper or illegal acts, and then they will be "square" and tell him that if he persists in it they may have to "snitch" for his own good, that it is to keep him from becoming a thief or some day getting into jail, so that they can make the boy feel that it is because of their loyalty to him and because they love him and because they want to keep him out of trouble rather than get him into trouble that they "snitch." It may be readily seen with men as well as boys, that if one stands by and watches his companions steal or afterwards participates in the fruits of the unlawful enterprise, and then turns informer, that such an individual would be looked upon with scorn and contempt, and so we recognize the good, the loyalty, the really noble impulses after all, back of the rules of the boys on these questions, but which are sometimes, though not often, perverted and misdirected for lack of understanding.

The result of the Saturday morning talk is that there is a better understanding, and if you want to handle boys you must understand them and they must understand you. This is too often not the case. I have talked to the boys on the subject of "ditching." If they do not like a boy they make it disagreeable for him to run with the crowd and when they do this they all say in Denver that he has been "ditched." "Cut it out" is a common expression among Denver boys. When boys are in the house at the table and with their parents and relatives or teachers and adults they will not, as a rule, use these terms, but with the boys they use nothing else in discussing such subjects.

SLANG TERMS.

I have been criticised for using these slang terms. I have repeatedly told the boys that they must use good English and not expect to use such slang terms; and they must be careful not to let the slang possess them; and I prefer that, in talking among themselves, they limit these terms to as few as possible. I believe this is preferable to trying to stamp out such things. It would be worse than useless to attempt it.

I do not believe there is one parent out of ten who has the slightest knowledge of the slang terms their boys constantly employ with their companions. Among boys a "jigger" (in Denver) is the boy who watches when they are up to some mischief. If anybody is coming they yell "jigger." The father of a certain boy from one of the weathiest and most refined homes in Denver, learned for the first time from his son, through my direction, that he had been in some serious trouble as to which the boy had tried to avoid responsibility with me by saying he was the "jigger." He had used the term constantly among his companions for years, but the father told me that he had never heard it before and supposed it referred to some kind of a bug. The greatest encouragement to the free use of slang is to know nothing about it and make no attempt by wise methods to overcome it or rather to see that it is limited. What man is there who did not use such terms when he was a boy?—only using different words to express the same meaning. I know I did. It is a good deal like boy nicknames. It would be foolish to try to prevent it; as a rule it does not hurt us; we get over it, and it can all be employed judiciously to get the confidence and interest of the boy. We have found, after four years' experience, that the judicious use of a few of their slang terms not only does not hurt the boy, but actually helps him and wins his confidence, and with such wisdom and discretion as may be brought to bear, we shall continue at times when it is deemed necessary, to talk to the boys to a certain extent much the same as they talk with one another. I do not think it would be a good thing for parents or school teachers to do, and the boys understand perfectly, when I do this, that it is not because of any habit or desire or intention to encourage it, but because of my sympathy for them in the rather different relation I occupy, and it gives me a hold upon many of them that I could not get in any other way. Again, it depends upon the individual who employs such methods. Some attempting this might do it so injudiciously as to work injury rather than good.

THE WORD OF CHEER.

After the Saturday morning talks the boys are called up in groups, alphabetically—no names are called out publicly in Court. In talking, it is "Willie" and "John" and "Tom," and as they are talked to in groups of eight or ten, there is no danger of getting the Willie's and Tom's and John's mixed. If the report is "good," as over 90 per cent. of them are, I always express my joy and satisfaction with a pat on head, a shake of the hand, a slap on the shoulder,—turn to the rest of the boys and tell them what a bully fellow John is; that he is "one of the squarest kids that ever lived;" that he is a trump, and then when he has gone, to the delight of the other boys, I may recall him and say, "Johnnie, my boy, I told those people (referring generally to the complainants) that you were a good boy, and that you would more than make up for any mistakes you had made and now you have shown me that I was right, that I told the truth; now don't you ever make me out a liar;" of course, John's face is wreathed in smiles and the other boys just "tickled to death."

The Juvenile Law says that its purpose is to treat the child not as a criminal but as needing aid, encouragement and assistance, and so the whole proceeding is as near as possible one of joy, and no boy is afraid—except to do wrong. It is not a question of leniency as some mistakenly suppose. It is simply the best way to bring out, to encourage the good and suppress the evil. Of course, there are sometimes disappointments, but where there is one this way there are ten the other way. I have in mind that six months ago a certain school boy who had been scolded, nagged and whipped was brought to Court and became a splendid fellow, obedient and ambitious under the report system. A boy rebels not so much against authority as ignorant authority. Of course, there is firmness through it all, but the kind that commands respect and does not respond with hate. Again, particular cases vary this proceeding and make it a work of constant interest. I always tell some good point in a particular boy to the little group around me and it makes all the boys proud and glad. Sometimes it is how we got "the laugh on the cop" because Frank became good and "cut it out"; how we got the best of the school attendance officer because Tom kept his word with me and was on the square and stayed in school—as most of the chronic little truants do, after they have reached the Juvenile Court and the reporting system.

OBJECTION TO REPORT SYSTEM.

And yet, I have heard people who never attended our Court say that the report system in Denver is objectionable because it permitted boys to come together and because of association it was bad. If this remark was made to anyone who had habitually visited our Juvenile Court they could hardly have patience to do more than denounce it as nonsense. I do not mean to underestimate the importance of association. I have noticed that in the larger cities the boys of the Juvenile Court seem harder, as a type, than in Denver, and it might not work there. It depends for its success on many things and might not succeed in other cities as in Denver. Of course, there may be exceptional cases where association of this kind in Denver may have worked an injury on an individual boy, but the great advantages derived more than compensate for any such exceptional bad effect, and if we should abolish the report system because of association we should have to abolish all the schools for the same reason, for I know schools in Denver—and, of course, I know it is true in every other city—where there are from fifty to one-hundred boys who have committed thefts; where there are hundreds who swear and tell obscene stories, and others have been affected by it, and yet they are allowed to play in the school yards with other children and no one has suggested for this reason that we abolish the public schools. If this be a reason for abolishing the report system, then let us be consistent and keep them out of school where association is constant, shut them up in hot-houses, and have a race of "sissies" and "milk sops." We do not want to make a boy a "tough" on the one hand or a "weakling" on the other. Our aim is to make each individual boy strong enough in himself and in his own character, to avoid the wrong and do the right, because it is right and best for him.

DIFFICULTIES OF REPORT SYSTEM.

If a boy forgets his report on Saturday morning he must come back Monday at 5 o'clock when the Judge comes from the bench and either see him or a probation officer. If he fails to report without good excuse he may be detained in the Detention School over Sunday when he would prefer to be out at play. If the report is poor the boy generally gives an indication of sorrow and promises to make it better the next time. The list of these poor reports is carefully kept and upon the next report day, if he has kept his resolution, there is a special word of praise, and thus his character is strengthened and the boy is subjected neither to anger nor violence. If it is poor a second time he is put upon some week-day "five o'clock docket," which means a private interview with the Judge when he comes from the bench. I take the boy into my chambers alone. I try to find out why he gets "poor." I learn all about his school life, what he thinks of his teacher, I listen to his own freely expressed explanations, I tell him how anxious I am to have him "stay with me," how I want to "stay with him" through thick and thin; how I want him to be my friend because I want to be his, and therefore that it is not square with his teacher or with me that he should continue to get "poor." That I do not want to "send him up" to Golden unless he compels it. But this must be the result if he insists, etc. This often produces good results. Now, because a boy has a "poor" report does not mean that he has committed any serious offense; it simply means that he has violated some rule of discipline in the school which he promised to rigidly obey as the good which would overcome the evil he has done.

HOW THE SCHOOLS WORK WITH THE COURT.

Some of the teachers in Denver will take a special interest in such a boy and when they do it helps us wonderfully. There are very few of the teachers who do not appreciate and enter into the spirit of the thing, but I am sorry to say there are some. Some of them regard it as rather an imposition to even write the reports, and I have had boys tell me, and on investigation have found it to be true, that the teacher would flippantly say they had no time to write reports. I remember one case where a teacher said that it was a nuisance to write reports for two boys in her room.

It was not long before they were excused at her request. I did not think they should have been excused, but in order to test it I let them go, and within a month they were returned to the Juvenile Court. If the interest in those two boys had been sincere at both ends of the line this might not have happened.

By arrangement with the superintendent of compulsory education in Denver, we have sent to the Court on Friday afternoon, before the Saturday when the boys report, a statement from the principals of the different schools of the boys on probation, detailing their conduct and school attendance so that we know Saturday morning at the meeting of the Court just what the records are. But, notwithstanding this, each boy is made responsible to receive from his teacher his report and bring it in person when he comes to the Court and present it to the Judge as he comes with a little squad under the letter of the alphabet with which his last name begins.

On the Monday morning succeeding Juvenile Court day, Mrs. Gregory, the lady probation officer who sits at the desk and keeps the records and is in communication by telephone with every school in Denver, makes up the list of the probationers. This list is printed under the headings of the different schools in the city arranged alphabetically. It is the probation list of the school boys reporting to the Juvenile Court and for private circulation only among the principals of the schools having probationers. This informs the principals as to who the boys are in his or her school reporting to the Court and enables them to give special care and attention to those particular boys. Very often, but not always, they demand and are entitled to more care, more patience, more attention, more sympathy, more love, and more firmness than the other boys. And where they are given this by the teacher, it makes it easier for the Court.

HOW THE "CAUSES" COME OUT IN THE GRIND.

By this grinding out process, as these boys come through the Court with their reports, we soon hit upon the weak cases and then proceed with care and patience to ascertain the defect. Of course, there are a great many causes that often contribute to bring about the results and these will be treated under another head. We try to study that boy as a skilled physician would study his patient. The child is sick—not physically but morally. Normally he is good. We have before us not a bad child, not a criminal. We have before us an individual in the chrysalis, being formed. We want to assist in the formation. There is really nothing yet to *reform*. It may be that the formation has been going wrong for years. It may have begun with lax discipline, weakness and leniency on the one hand, or brutality on the other, in the home. If the trouble is in the home, the parents are sent for and long, earnest consultations are held in the Judge's chambers. The probation officer may visit the home or take an interest kindly and firmly in order that the evil may be overcome. Very often the teacher is called in for consultation. A consultation more important even than those of wise and learned physicians over some physical ailment of the child, when everyone is ready to become a hero to preserve his life. His morals, his soul, his future as a citizen, and possibly a parent is a great deal more important. If he dies that is the end of our responsibility. If he lives no man knows what may be the end of his influence, of his power in this world for good or evil; and so a morally sick child is of infinitely more importance, demands infinitely more attention, care, solicitude, patience, kindness and firmness than a physically sick child. Of course, both demand attention and care, but the trouble is, in the past physical ailments have received all the skill and moral ailments have not only been neglected but brutally treated. It would be much worse to take a wayward child to some of the jails in which I have seen them steeped in corruption, as the first step to correct their faults, than to take your sick child to the city garbage dump and leave it abandoned, alone and unattended. So the Juvenile Court, when it comes to those cases that continue to report "poor" in this regular and systematic grind, puts them in our hospital or operating room, as it were.

THE PHYSICIAN AND THE COURT.

By this system physical defects are often found to be the cause of moral delinquency, and so we have a physical department in connection with the Juvenile Court. Johnny has been a stupid, dull boy, and brought poor reports. We find that his eyes are poor, his vision defective. They said he was "poor" or "bad" because no one knew, no one was interested enough to find out, no one cared. I remember well little Eddie who was recommended for the Industrial School because he was rebellious and had been suspended from school, and therefore went to the street and drifted into idleness and thence into crime, but Eddie came to this mill in the Juvenile Court and he was ground through with the rest, but he came out "poor." He was in the wrong hopper. We tried it again and I discovered in a few hours' talk with him one afternoon, that he was "strange and peculiar" as his teacher had declared, but she never divined the cause. Perhaps she could not. I sent Eddie to the doctor. He found that he had had fits when he was seven years old and the nervous trouble had returned in a different form at twelve and this was what made him peevish, bull-headed and rebellious. Was Eddie to blame for all this? He was placed under treatment. At the end of eight months the teacher, who declared a year before, meaning well of course, that there was no hope for Eddie this side of the Industrial School, wrote a beautiful letter admitting her error and saying that Eddie was the best boy in the school. Here the two surgeons, moral and physical, had come together in the interest of the child, and their work was good and the results were good.

PURE CUSSEDNESS.

Sometimes the diagnosis from the physical department is "pure cussedness," even though the moral department may deny this and say, "weakness, misfortune, misunderstood."

SKILL REQUIRED.

It has been said that skill in evoking melody from the harp is as nothing compared with skill in arousing the nobler impulses of the soul and bringing out its most energetic faculties, and so we find very often an instrument so out of tune, so discordant, that there is no master to put it back where God intended it, and where it was originally. If we have failed, perhaps some one else will not fail, and then perhaps that some one else cannot be found. Too often we haven't the time, because that time is demanded by so many cases. So we realize that there is a limitation to what may be done this side of the Industrial School. It may be that the home is so bad, or so helpless, or

that there is no home at all, and occasionally, for the sake of enforcing discipline and furnishing an example, a boy must be sent
to the Industrial School, but if there is a home, that generally
is the place for him, and the best fight is won when we can keep
him there and correct him there.

THE TEACHER AND THE BOY.

I remember, during one school year, as a result of these talks
with certain eight boys in Chambers (who had brought "poor"
reports), I became satisfied that they hated their teachers. The
man or woman who has incurred the hate of a child is a hopeless factor in its handling, as a rule. It does not always mean
that because a boy is unruly or a teacher or parent fails, or that
we fail, that we have incurred the hate of the boy. The failure
may be attributed to entirely different causes, but we must try
as best we can, to find the true cause. There are many different
causes and they vary with different cases, and require the most
careful study and earnest interest in every case. And so I became satisfied that the cause of the trouble in these eight cases
was the antipathy between the child and teacher. It was entirely immaterial who might be responsible for this condition.
The teacher may have been excusable, but not likely. The fault
may have been entirely with the child, but not likely. The fact
remains that there was hate and rebellion. Why was it that
three of these boys had excellent reports right along the year before under a different teacher? I got those boys changed, shifted
around to different schools, and, with one exception, each brought
excellent reports until they were finally discharged. I believe
the eighth boy would have turned out well under some other
teacher, but at the end of the school year he finished the eighth
grade, and he has been exemplary and satisfactory in every way
in reporting as a working boy. He was discharged, after prov-
ing to be the best one of the eight. It has now been over
two years since this experiment was made. One of the best
of these boys I had, at the recommendation of the school attendance officer, the principal of the school and others, actually
committed to the Industrial School (it was before the days of the
detention school), and he had been placed in jail until the officer
could take him there. I shall never regret the visit I made to the

jail one Sunday afternoon and the changing of my mind and revocation of the commitment and the adoption of the plan of changing his school *at home* and not to Golden (where the State Industrial School is located).

THE ATTENDANCE OFFICER AND THE PROBATION OFFICER.

All of this work would be practically impossible without the report system. The principal of each school being supplied every two weeks with the names of the probationers, in case the probationers fail to show up in school it is immediately telephoned to headquarters of the Juvenile Court, and one of the field officers (the two men probation officers), would be detailed to look up the boy. Of course the time of informing the Court depends upon the particular boy. The principal of the school might be so familiar with his home and have such confidence in the boy that he would assume that there was a good excuse, but if no excuse appeared within 24 hours the unalterable rule between the schools and the Court is that it must be reported at the probation office. In case of a boy who has not been to the Juvenile Court, failing to appear in school, the principal would notify the superintendent of compulsory education and one of the school attendance officers from that department would be detailed to investigate and report upon the case. The parents would first be warned by a notice from the attendance officer of their duty, and only in case the home failed to correct the faulty school attendance would it be brought to the Court and turned over to the probation department.

REPORTS OF WORKING BOYS. EMPLOYERS AND EMPLOYMENT.

There are generally an average of about thirty working boys upon probation, brought in upon petitions filed by the probation officers. These cases are treated exactly as those of school boys except that they are not required to report if it will interfere with their work. For their accommodation and convenience, an evening session is held in chambers at which the Judge is often present and those boys who can come are encouraged to come. The entire proceeding is then one of friendly inquiry as to how the boys are getting along and it frequently happens that we learn much of their troubles, when a kindly word of advice or encouragement is given. It was difficult at first to get employers to see that there is really very little difference, with a few exceptions, between a boy who has been caught in some mischief or has committed some offense which makes it necessary to bring him into Court, and other boys. Where this is explained and understood we have been gratified to find, on the part of many employers, a disposition to give more encouragement, comfort, sympathy and assistance to boys who have fallen into error than those who have not, or at least who have not been caught. If every boy in the city between ten and sixteen years of age was caught and proceeded against by the one whose rights he violates, or by some officer called upon to enforce the law, for every offense committed, there would be very few who would escape the Juvenile Court. We therefore do everything in our power to abolish any distinction of mark or identity upon any boy who has been in the Juvenile Court. Of course there are a few exceptional cases as to which this rule might be considered questionable, but the purpose should always be to serve the best interests of the greatest number of boys who reach the Juvenile Court and who are, I repeat, no more or less than average boys, no better or no worse. I prefer to regard the matter in this light as to the majority of so-called delinquents. The exceptional cases may be taken care of differently and yet in a way that will not do an injury or an injustice to the average case. And so we feel justified in the course here indicated; and the answer to any criticisms or doubt concerning it is simply this, that any other course would warrant more doubt, more criticism, and in the end work injustice in more cases. One great mistake that some employers make is in thinking that if a boy recommended by the Juvenile Court fails to give satisfaction, they should attribute it to the fact that he has been in the Juvenile Court, and classify all other boys similarly situated with him, and thus impose a hardship on a boy who has been in the Juvenile Court which is without justification. If such an employer would only stop to think he would find that, in his experience, other boys had failed to give satisfaction also who had never been in the Juvenile Court, and who might, because of abundant energy and natural animal spirits—producing great industry when rightly directed, but bringing them to the Juvenile Court when wrongly directed—have given greater satisfaction had they actually been in the Juvenile Court. Some of the manliest, best boys that ever lived have been in the Denver Juvenile Court. I say this not to encourage or to furnish an excuse for other boys coming there, but as more than justified for the protection of those who have been there; and I could at the same time properly say that some of the worst boys I ever knew have been in the Juvenile Court; and some of the worst boys I ever knew have not been in the Juvenile Court. What we should do is to foster as far as possible a spirit of charity in dealing with such matters, and at the same time not encourage thereby a spirit of indifference as to whether one does or does not become a charge of this court. Everything possible should be done to keep boys out of the Juvenile Court and to impress upon them the undesirability of such a result, and all of this can be done while at the same time we throw an arm of protection and a mantle of charity about those with whom the Court must necessarily deal; because it is our duty in correcting the boy for his good and the good of the State, to do him just as little harm as possible by the process and yet secure the enforcement of the law and his redemption to good citizenship. We shall not do this if, at the time of his correction, we weigh him down and handicap him with difficulties that make his lot harder than it was before the Court intervened in his behalf. Only where an employer seems to take an interest in the boy and we know it can do the boy no possible harm do we receive reports from employers, and it is never done without the consent of the boy. We do not want any boy to have the slightest occasion to feel that we find it necessary that he should be watched, and the report system, as it is conducted, is entirely free from any suggestion of espionage. Its true purpose in this respect has already been explained, and it is thoroughly understood by the boys and can not become offensive.

REPORTS DURING SCHOOL VACATION.

For school boys, during the summer vacation, we have "report-day" once a month when the boys give their own reports verbally and we take their word for it. If they have been in any mischief that may be termed lawlessness, they always tell us about it, and I have had them mark themselves "poor" with a promise to do better—a promise invariably kept.

TIME OF PROBATION AND RULES.

We have no rules for the period of probation. It depends on each individual case, on the home, the neighborhood, the environment, as well as the particular type of boy. A great many things must enter into the case and it would be absurd, in our opinion, to attempt to enforce definite rules. A boy from a good home, whose parents are amply able to enforce obedience and care for him after he has learned a sufficient lesson for a violation of law, may properly be excused after a few months of reporting if the reports are satisfactory. A boy from half a home or no home, bad environment, constantly beset by temptations and surrounded by evil influences, might bring equally as good reports for the same period of time, and yet not be excused. We have never had a complaint from a boy or the slightest suspicion of injustice aroused in their minds because of this condition. They are all well satisfied that what is done is for their good and they appreciate better than might generally be expected all of the rules of the Juvenile Court because they have been frequently spoken of to them in the Saturday morning talks. The Court will not excuse a school boy from reporting unless it is on the recommendation of the principal of the school. In case it is recommended, however, by the school principal, it then becomes a matter of discretion with the Judge, and if not excused on such recommendation, it is usually because the Judge and probation officers are familiar with some phase of the case of which the principal does not know, and because such refusal is considered for the best interest of the boy. This is duly explained to the principal in order that no misunderstanding may arise. But such cases are very exceptional.

CLASSIFICATION OF CASES.

Anyone dealing with Juvenile Court work must readily appreciate that the offenses of children, because of the various causes and motives actuating them, should be broadly classified in order to be more intelligently dealt with.

1. MISCHIEVOUS CHILDREN.

Probably the least harmful class of cases, and yet, sometimes, the most annoying and really dangerous, if permitted to continue, may properly be attributed to mischief, the love of fun and adventure. These things in child life are just as natural as hunger. It becomes necessary, in a city especially, where it is practically impossible to notify all the parents of those offending and where a large number of them, if notified, would as indignantly deny the charge as their guilty boys, to bring in many boys for what is innocent enough from the boy's standpoint, but often very serious from the standpoint of others. A few illustrations of this class of cases in Denver may be given. Hooking on cars, putting rocks in the switches to see the car "shoot the sidetrack," wiring up the signal boxes at the terminals of the car lines in very respectable suburbs of the city, in order to be "shagged" (chased) by the conductor, or as one boy explained to me "to hear the motorman cuss;" jerking trolleys, greasing the tracks on the hills, occasional throwing rocks, eggs, vegetables, etc., at the passing tramway cars much to the delight of the boys and the discomforture of the passengers; breaking electric light globes, breaking windows, going into vacant houses and committing more or less depredation, playing ball in the streets down town, taking ice cream and other tempting edibles from the back porches of the neighbors, shooting "beanies" and small firearms in the city limits, etc. From the boy's standpoint all of this is fun and amusement. Yet they know it is wrong, and they are very careful not to get caught at it. These things are bad enough in themselves and are really the most prolific source of complaint from citizens. I have known boys of some of the best families, many of them having good fathers and mothers, who have become chronically engaged in deviltry of this kind, and often where efforts had been made through the school, with the parents, and with others, to break it up, without avail, it becomes absolutely necessary, for the example to other boys and in order to check it before it so blunts the moral sense of the boy that it becomes serious lawlessness or incipient criminality, to bring them to the Juvenile Court.

HOW THE HOME AND THE SCHOOL HELP.

We have corrected a great many of these troubles through the home and school, without the direct intervention of the Court, and yet there would be no limit to the juvenile lawlessness of this character if the boys were not sometimes brought to the Court. In my opinion, while the homes and schools can do much, they are really powerless to entirely prevent this class of mischief, or keep it within bounds, without the aid of the Court. It always has existed to a certain extent and it always will.

HOW THE CITY AND COUNTRY BOYS DIFFER.

In the country, or in the country town, if the boy invades the watermelon patch or the apple orchard, the neighbor can inform the father, and the father can deal with the boy in the cellar or the barn, in his own peculiar way. In the city the situation is entirely different.

COURT NECESSARY IN MISCHIEVOUS CASES.

There are a great many neighbors of such delinquents who suffer in their property and sometimes their person by these depredations. They do not always care to take the matter up with parents. They may live next door and not know them. I have also known some kindly disposed neighbors to attempt this who were simply rebuked for their pains while the parents would take the side of the child instead of correcting him, and thus encourage lying and deception in the child, cause bad feeling in the neighborhood, and so make the case a great deal worse.

ALL TO BE TREATED ALIKE.

Again, the success of law enforcement depends upon treating all alike. In some sections of the city, where the population is more congested, among the poorer classes, the parents may be away at work with no one to look after the children except the attendance officer or probation officer who already have more than they can do. Such parents, because of industrial conditions, really need help with their children. Often it is the case that the father has deserted the mother and without the firmness of a father's care the boy is running out at nights with the "wild kids" in the neighborhood and the efforts of the mother are absolutely fruitless. It would soon cause a feeling of distrust for the laws and the court if this class of boys were brought to the Juvenile Court and another class, among parents and in neighborhoods more fortunately situated, were allowed to go without the restraint of the law. I know a certain boy from the slums who was arrested for stealing a bicycle. He sold the bicycle for sufficient money to treat the gang to ice cream. He knew that certain boys on Capitol Hill were taking ice cream from the back porches. He naively said to me: "Judge, if our neighbors were rich enough to keep ice cream on the back porches we wouldn't have to swipe wheels to get money to buy something good." The motives for both of these offences were exactly the same. The methods of gratifying a natural desire for a good time were simply different because of the different environment. The treatment was entirely different. The poor boy who stole the wheel in order to get ice cream lay in a filthy jail for two weeks, charged with a penitentiary offence, and stigmatized and brutalized as a burglar, at the age of 12, while the boys who went on their neighbors' porches and took the ice cream from exactly the same motive, were looked upon very much as the country boy who goes after his neighbor's fruit. Of course, the poor boy was wrongly treated. Forty others were differently treated and corrected without any jail and are all good boys now. The boy who was thus put in jail did not quit at all. It is simply an illustration of how the State, by its brutal, blind methods of treating these questions in the past, has made more criminals than it has ever reformed, and admonishes us of the necessity for more intelligent and sane treatment of such cases. Of course, such children should be corrected, but at the same time they must be protected. In the Juvenile Court they are not charged with crime at all.

MISCHIEVOUS CASES EASILY CORRECTED.

For such offences they are generally easily enough corrected. The Court experience and realization of the restraining hand of the law, the lesson learned as to where fun ends and the law begins, is entirely sufficient, and while probably most of such city boys would become good men if simply left to home training, even without this court experience, yet it is certain a large per cent. would not. No one knows what boys will make up this per cent., consequently all must be amenable to the law. We should make no distinctions. It is indeed the satisfaction of natural desires unlawfully among children that is the very inception of criminality, and if permitted to continue unchecked, is sure to produce evil results. Several hundred boys from all classes of homes and parents in Denver (some our very best people) have been brought to the Juvenile Court for this class of offences. Not one of them was ever returned for its repetition. At the Saturday morning talks I have often spoken to these boys of the danger of what I tell them is "having fun in an unlawful manner." I explain to them the rights of others and the respect they owe to the law intended for the protection of all, and their duty as little citizens to keep their neighborhood clean and its reputation above reproach, to banish lawlessness from their midst, to be good boys, not "goody boys," and yet not rowdies and school toughs, which surely leads to lawlessness in the end, for which there is no excuse.

BOYS BEST HELP IN MISCHIEVOUS CASES.

The boys themselves (as discussed in another part of this report) have done more to prevent this kind of lawlessness than the civil authorities in those neighborhoods where it has been worst and where we have succeeded in organizing the boys for law enforcement and decency.

2. CHILDREN WHO ARE TOO WEAK TO RESIST TEMPTATION.

I have known some splendid boys, really good boys, from good homes, to commit an occasional theft, much to the surprise of their parents. This is often shocking, because of its infrequency and inconsistency with the life of the child. The boy naturally likes to have a good time. He wants to go to the theater, the natatorium, or the gardens with other boys who have spending money when he has none. I know a splendid type of boyhood as a good illustration of this. He comes from one of the most respectable homes in Denver. As a messenger from a certain store he was sent to another store with a package containing money. The business man was not in and he returned once or twice, and the oftener he returned the stronger grew the temptation to keep the money. He finally told a story to the effect that a lady in the office, whom he supposed was the stenographer, had told him to leave the package with her and he had left it. He told this story after a petition was filed in the Juvenile Court. The business man was sure that a certain lady, whom he suspected, had been in the office and had led the boy to believe that she was employed there, so suspicion was diverted to the woman. Everyone believed the boy's story, and I was requested to dismiss the case. I knew the moment I spoke to the lad that he was guilty. I told his mother and father so, much to their chagrin and almost indignation, for the boy had fine certificates of character from every one who ever knew him, including his teachers, employers and friends. I took the boy to my chambers and without a particle of proof, described to him almost exactly what had happened. He promptly confessed to me the entire transaction and subsequently earned and returned the money and is one of the princeliest little fellows I know at this time. I know a number of such cases among children of the poor, where the boys have had an untarnished reputation and never have been guilty of any serious offense until overcome by temptations under trying circumstances. Such cases are not confined to children of any class. What such boys need generally is sympathy and encouragement and the kind of interest in them that will strengthen the character. I have always found them full of sorrow and genuine repentance. I do not recall a case where such an offense was ever repeated.

3. CHILD VICTIMS OF INCOMPETENT· PARENTS.

Careless and incompetent parents are by no means confined to the poor. In fact, in my experience, the most blameworthy of such parents are among the so-called business men and prominent citizens.

TOO MUCH EASE, MONEY AND GOOD TIME.

They seem to think their duty is ended when they have debauched the boy with luxury and the free use of money. They permit him to fill his life with a round of pleasure, and let him satiate his appetite without knowing what he is doing or whither he is drifting. They are too busy to become his chum or companion, and so he soon develops a secret and private life which is often filled with corruption, and because of his standing or influence and money, he may be kept out of the courts or the jails, but nevertheless is eventually added to society as a more dangerous citizen than many men who have been subjected to both. A captain of police in a large city recently said to me that he had investigated in six weeks twenty-four cases of embezzlement by young men in business houses, but because they were of good families and the father had settled no prosecution was had. A financially well-to-do father once said to me that he was too busy to look after his boys, to be companionable or take an interest in them. We have no more dangerous citizens than such men. This is too often the case. In the end, I believe such a man would profit more by less business and better boys. This man was rearing a son who would lead a profligate life, squandering the money he had accumulated, because of too much "business" to look after the boy. The idleness, ease and corruption wrought in society generally by such boys and young men, and so the consequent suffering and misery, is infinitely more inexcusable, more general, far reaching and dangerous than that wrought by average thieves and burglars, or the class of boys who are degenerated by opposite conditions, such as lack of nourishment and sufficient money to enjoy any of the common pleasures of life. Our most dangerous citizens are by no means confined to those who are or have been in prison.

BAD EXAMPLES.

Then there are parents who are intemperate, shiftless or dishonest, and because of this condition and the bad example constantly furnished them, the boys really have no home. Such children could hardly be expected to keep out of the Juvenile Court. Again, both parents are often absolutely unfit to have children, and if it were possible, should have been denied the right or opportunity. Such cases are often extremely difficult to handle upon probation for the lack of any decent home influences.

LACK OF COMPANIONSHIP.

There is another class of really respectable and industrious parents who mean well, who are firm, or, rather, stern and too often cross and grouchy, without sympathy or companionship for their children. They never allow them any money to spend, and deny them things that other children have. In other homes there is nagging and constant fault-finding, never seeing any good in the boy and unintentionally but positively stultifying the good that is in him, and bringing out all the evil of which he is capable. There is the impatient, selfish, angered or brutal parent on the one hand, and the weak, vacillating, lenient parent on the other, and between these extremes many a boy goes down.

RAILROAD CASES.

Under the head of incompetent parents I would also group those cases which are, especially in the cities, of so much annoyance to railroad companies. It is a certain class of parents who are to blame. The children are encouraged to go upon the railroad tracks and steal coal from the cars. They find a certain justification in their poverty to do this, yet it is extremely blighting to the conscience and morals. Such children, even at a tender age, soon learn to avoid the special officer and constantly have the "jigger" out to sound the note of warning when he heaves in sight. Thus they know they are doing wrong and are sustained in it by their parents, who, to their minds, are superior in every way to the detested officer. The next step is into the box car; the stealing of brass and other appliances which may be sold to junk dealers. Thus encouraged by their parents what they do is from their standpoint perfectly legitimate so long as they do not "get caught."

PROOF THAT PARENTS ARE TO BLAME.

In the last eighteen months there have been brought to the Juvenile Court a great number of parents, some junk dealers and others, for contributing to the delinquency of this class of children, and while there were twenty odd cases of brass stealing and similar depredations about the tracks and cars of the railroad companies during the first three months of the Juvenile Court of Denver, there has not been a single case of this character during the past 18 months. This clearly demonstrated that the trouble was with the adults and not with the children, yet in most courts it is the children and not the adults who are brought in, with the result that the children feel that they are the victims of persecution, and the trouble is not diminished but continued with increasing bitterness and hatred towards the officers of the law so that eventually the children often have no respect for officers or courts.

JUVENILE ANARCHISTS.

From this class are constantly recruited a dangerous type of juvenile anarchists. By bringing in the parents and putting the responsibility upon them, the parents are compelled to order the children to desist from such practices, and receiving their orders and instructions from the parents the offense is prevented and there is no hatred for the State. In this way incipient anarchy is checked. Until one has studied this question and observed the alarming number of such cases in the cities there can not begin to be any just appreciation of the tremendous importance of this one detail of the child problem.

4.   ENVIRONMENT AND ASSOCIATION.

These causes are of infinitely more importance, in my opinion, than all others combined, because they more or less involve them all. I know four boys who, under other conditions, might be princely little fellows; yet, the handsome, blue-eyed one of 12, who would make a picture for an artist, will deliberately plan to get a drunken man into an alley and rob him of his money. These boys live in the very worst part of the city where there are cheap dives and saloons of the lowest order. If you get their confidence they will tell you glibly about drunken men and laugh and joke about it as a matter of course. They will talk of the respective merits of different dives, and tell you of the fights they have seen there, and the boys whom they know who have been drunk because they purchased the liquor in these places. Many of them have witnessed shooting scrapes, and we only recently prosecuted men for selling them firearms. The result is they are constantly surrounded by bad examples. One of them goes to the saloon for liquor (or did before we began to prosecute the men who permitted them to come into the saloon) for others, though he may detest the stuff himself. He may not be a drunkard. Yet he already is a thief (to the criminal law) and a dangerous example of juvenile depravity. He is not so likely to be ruined by liquor as by the example of those who have been ruined by liquor. I have made a companion of this child and in our walks and talks I have learned more than I could have from a book. This source of degradation and pollution to childhood is almost impossible to eradicate, but, of course, it is generally confined to that portion of the city where the population is congested and opportunities for association and observation of crooks and criminals is constantly present. The only hope generally is to lift the child out of it. Thus it comes that children from such environment are the ones most frequently committed to the Industrial School.

WHAT TO DO.

Under the Colorado law we try to improve this environment by impressing upon parents, citizens and others a responsibility for these children, and so we have had in court a man who would send one of these children to the saloon as well as the bar-keeper who filled the can. Children of this class are most likely to be those of real criminal tendencies. They have very little respect for men, because they have seen too much of the evil side of men. They have too often heard their father curse their mother or have seen him beat her. Profanity and obscenity is no longer revolting to them, because soul and conscience have been hardened to these things. They are too often sneaks and extremely deceptive. Anything is justifiable so long as they do not get "caught." I have found this class of children to be the hardest to appeal to. They are often apparently totally lacking in any sense of responsibility. There is no pride to which you can appeal. Kindness is too often looked upon as weakness. The truth is, their little souls are absolutely stunted, deformed. For such children the detention school offers little in the way of discipline. It is simply better than the jail, which soon loses its terrors. Yet some remarkable successes have been made with some of the worst of such children, and what I have said here pertains to such children as I have seen in crowded districts of other cities rather than in Denver, where we have fewer cases of the type here described. Yet I have sent a boy of this type to the Indnstrial School alone, when I had feared that I might only excite his contempt and ridicule as I should had I failed to arouse those nobler impulses of the soul which are certainly there, but so dormant, so paralyzed by environment and example as to seem almost incapable of being aroused. We should by no means despair of such a case. The object in removing such boys to the Industrial School is to take them away from those sights which have made such base impressions until time and better influences shall bring about an awakening. I have known some boys of this type, after three or four years in the Industrial School, to come out absolutely changed for the better and who are well on the way to good citizenship.

5. BOY BUMS AND RUNAWAYS.

What we term the "moving about fever" is as sure to come in the lives of some children as the measles. I have observed that the great number of such children who come under my observation in the Juvenile Court are those whose homes are in the vicinity of the railroad yards, yet I have known some persistent little runaways who come from homes in the best parts of the city. The spirit of adventure, the desire to see the world, impressions coming to the mind from seeing the trains boom in and out of the city, the wondering induced as to the places and cities from whence they come and whither they go, seem to take hold upon the childish mind, and unless checked and controlled may add him eventually to the army of vagrants and tramps that infest the country.

I once tried a rather doubtful experiment with such a boy. He was an habitual runaway and eighteen months in the Industrial School had not effected a cure. I succeeded in getting him to come and tell me when he was going to run away. He came one day as though possessed with a fever and said he must "take a ride." I deliberately gave him permission to bum his way to Colorado Springs on condition that he would go no farther and would come back within a week. I knew that he was fully capable of going to California or the Gulf of Mexico, whence he had often "taken a ride." Of course, I took chances, but I took an equally desperate chance if I returned him to the Industrial School, which had already failed to cure the malady. The boy was as good as his word, and, after two experiences of this kind, now two years ago, he has ceased to be a bum and is in every way promising. I know a splendid little fellow who has a good home and father—poor, but honest and industrious people. He very much prefers running away and sleeping two or three months in piano boxes and the "fans" of the big buildings down town to staying at home.

Perhaps other classifications of children's cases might be made.

CAUSES.

Among the causes of delinquency which should be carefully considered by those called upon to work with the child problem in cities may be mentioned:

LAX ENFORCEMENT OF THE LAWS INTENDED FOR THE PROTECTION OF CHILDREN.

I believe that with few exceptions the police departments of the various cities are notoriously guilty of neglect in this respect, though a much better condition in this regard now exists in Denver than in most cities. This is largely due to indecent politics in the police department. An experienced police captain, for whom I have a high respect, declared as much to me. As he expressed it, when I asked him why it was that policemen would stand in front of a saloon and let the children flock in and out and see the sights they must see: "Why," said he, "they know nothing about it at headquarters, and the officer is expected to bring in his precinct delegation at the next convention and he needs the help of the saloon-keeper to do it. If he does not do it, he is liable to lose his job, and so the saloon-keeper is the boss of the policemen." I have had boys ask me if the policemen let the saloons remain open all day Sunday when it was against the law, why they could not steal things. If those who are called upon to enforce the law set such examples, what can we expect of children? One good example in a child's life is more important than all the preaching he can hear.

615398 A

DIVORCE, DESERTION, DRINK, AND, OF COURSE, DAMNATION OF THE HOME.

Every child born into the world starts as an irresponsible being. He has the divine right to be trained in the way he should go, and the persons who should do this are the parents. I believe that over half of the children brought to the Juvenile Court for offenses other than those denominated "mischievous cases" are practically homeless—that is, there has been a divorce or desertion in the family and the child has been denied his birthright. The result is the child must suffer and the State must suffer.

CASES CLASSIFIED. CAUSES CONSIDERED.

The officers of the Juvenile Court have dealt with the children coming there with due regard to all of these important questions, and the best success of this work will depend largely upon a complete understanding of their relation to the particular case and a due regard for the classification and causes herein referred to in order that the case may be intelligently and wisely treated.

BATHS AND LITERATURE.

In the basement of the Court House, adjoining the boiler room, is the bath room, about twenty feet square. Attached to the ceiling of this room are long pipes extending from one end to the other, with a cement pool in the middle. The effect is what is known with us as a "rain bath." We especially encourage those boys who have no such facilities in the home, to go through the bath room, and upon every Juvenile Court day from fifty to one hundred boys take the shower baths. In the Saturday morning talks I like to speak in special commendation of these boys. It is really the only chance that many of them have, and it is our intention to urge upon the school board that they supply similar baths in the schools situated among the homes of the poorer children.

The "American Boy" and "Young Americans" and "Success" are distributed among the boys each month, and no Juvenile Court boy, who is "on the square," will take these things and read "dime (now two for 5 cents) novels."

TRUANT GANG

GANGS
LOOKING FOR TROUBLE

MISCHIEVOUS GANG

THE GANG.

Thomas Carlyle said somewhere that there is a gregarious or sheep-like tendency in mankind to flock together and have a leader. I believe that it is now generally recognized by all students of boyhood that the gang spirit is more or less a natural instinct that should be wisely controlled and directed rather than suppressed. As judge of the Juvenile Court of Denver during the last three years there has been no feature of what to me has been a very interesting experience that exceeded some studies we have made of the gang, for the gang must be studied to be understood. Gangs are either good or bad, but it is the bad gangs that contribute so much to bringing into court a certain class of cases that are quite typical. It is not uncommon for the probation officer to be face to face with the mischief wrought by the "Dirty Dozen" or "Noisy Nine." Often we have found in these gangs the tribal instinct that began too far back in the past to even try to define. The gang has its good as well as its bad qualities. These have been often discussed. I shall only attempt to refer to the gang qualities as we have had to deal with them in the correction of wayward childhood.

The Twenty-Second Street Gang may have its wars with the Thirty-Third Street Gang, and the Battle Ax Gang may continue its efforts to exterminate the Horse Shoe Gang (named after their favorite plug tobacco), and whatever may be the result of the battle as between each other the results of the conflict seldom reach the court. If the opposing gangs do not settle their own troubles one way they will another, without appeal to outsiders. It is when the gang comes in contact with the rights of citizens that the trouble begins. Left alone to itself, the gang has many good qualities. Who has not observed the loyalty of its members to each other? Who has not observed its rules and laws, founded generally on really ennobling instincts, which seem to control its very existence—laws as binding and effective on a boy's conduct towards his mates as any which control our own conduct! For instance, it is the unalterable law of the gang "thou shalt not snitch" (tell on one another). When the gang or some of its leaders or members get into court, which they frequently do, you are going to be compelled to a certain extent to respect its laws if you expect it to respect yours. The police department and every other civil authority for the suppression of crime has too often been compelled to acknowledge the shocking number of depredations directly chargeable to the gang. In my experience nine-tenths of such offenses are rather the result of misdirected energy, thoughtlessness, and a certain uncurbed exuberance which is a part of the life of every boy. It often finds expression in individual boys through the gang and would never be thought of or felt but for the gang. There is often a certain wild, uncontrollable energy let loose when individuals are congregated together. It is that spirit of the mob which urges the individual when collectively engaged to do things which might be even mad and unthought of to the individual alone. It promotes and sustains a spirit of daring that at times will break out in depredations or acts of violence, for which each individual member thereof is responsible before the law; yet had the individual been left alone, uncontrolled by the spirit of the gang, he would have escaped entirely. How often a boy, looking for some excuse for his delinquency, will resort to the subterfuge, "All the kids were in it;" "So and So proposed we go on the back porch for the ice cream or the turkey, and before I thought we were all there and away again." It is all well enough to treat such excuses lightly, but after all, from one standpoint they carry more justice than we are inclined to concede. I have not a particle of doubt that the individual child very often would never have committed the same offense if alone, or even with his chum; but for this and other reasons the boy is not as a matter of fact a thief or a burglar. He is the victim of an instinct which, however wild, is nevertheless natural. It is perfectly natural that he should flock with his mates, that he should follow the leader. He is going to do this in most cases without stopping to reason why, and if he does stop to reason why he is mighty likely to capitulate to the taunt that he is a "sissy boy," a "coward," or "has no sand." It is all very easy in our world, forgetting as we sometimes do the boy's world, thinking only of our laws and denying any excuse for the existence of his laws, to scold, criticise or abuse the boy. Of course the gang must be corrected, curbed and controlled, but when the officer succeeds in catching its one hapless member, if we are going to do justice we must recognize the instincts here referred to as well as the laws and rules that control the gang. We can do this and at the same time most successfully correct the boy. You are going to make very little headway unless you bear in mind that it is the spirit of the gang and the gang itself that most needs correction rather than the unfortunate boy who was "pinched." Of course the individual boy may in some cases be successfully corrected without regard to these things, but more success will be had if they are recognized. In school or out of school, when the gang has made trouble and somebody is caught we must be sure that in correcting the one who is caught we do not so offend the natural and justifiable laws of Boyville that at the same time we are helping more to make sneaks and traitors.

HOW THE CASE AGAINST THE CHILD MUST BE JUDGED.

Every case against a child, then, must be judged more from the standard of the child than from that of the man. It must be judged more from the standpoint of certain well-recognized laws and rules that control child life than from those that should control the lives of adults. In the Juvenile Court these two worlds meet, as it were; harmony prevails, and the case is viewed with due regard to each. No one can seriously expect a street boy of twelve to respect the law intended for the protection of the fruit vender in the same way that we have a right to expect the adult to respect a law of no higher sanctity or binding effect for the protection of the banker or the merchant in the possession of his money or property. Yet not technically but positively the law has to a large extent exacted the same respect from each, the same penalties for a lack thereof. The jarring and jangling we all admit as a result of such a condition in the case of the child is simply because we attempt to judge entirely different conditions by exactly the same rule. You might as well expect to successfully treat every disease by the same remedy. You might as well expect to cure a child, even though afflicted with the same illness as an adult, with the same doses, the same diet, and the same general treatment. I am perfectly aware that children (I refer to those under seventeen) are capable of committing and in the large cities are constantly committing shocking and surprising offences, often showing a cunning and an intelligence that would match that of the adept adult criminal. It simply shows that precocity in childhood may be for evil as well as good. I have handled a number of such cases and spent many hours in their study. I believe in every such case there is a cause for the effect, a reason for the result that is not far to trace in the majority of instances. However bad exceptional cases may be, they cannot affect the method here suggested for more intelligently dealing with juvenile offenders.

OFF FOR THE BEET FIELDS—THE GANG PROPERLY DIRECTED

Not only must the general rule in dealing with such offenders be different from that in dealing with adults, but to
achieve the most success we must carry the proposition further
for the same general reasons, and deal with every case rather
from the standpoint of that particular case than from that of
any law.

HOW THE JUVENILE COURT WORKS WITH THE BOYS AND THE BOYS WITH THE COURT.

No feature of the Juvenile work has been more beneficial
than the work with the boys. As an illustration of how the work
is carried on, one or two cases will suffice. Take a mischievous
case: Certain boys had been putting rocks in the switches and
upon the tracks of the city tramway. The result was several
cars had been ditched and the lives of passengers endan-
gered, much to the annoyance of the company as well as the trav-
eling public, and really greatly to the damage of the morals of
the boys. After much effort, four or five boys were caught. These
boys were brought to my chambers by the officer. I explained to
them that I wanted to relieve the officer and have them take the
matter up and help me to stop it.

ELEMENT OF INTEREST IN A BOY'S LIFE.

Of course, their interest was immediately aroused and interest is everything in a boy's life. It is the reason why he
plays so much harder than he works, as a rule. In the one
case he is interested, in the other he is not. So we work upon
this principle. It was "interest" largely that started the lawlessness and now it should be the thing to break it up. The only
difference is the channel in which it is directed. These boys were
soon made to understand the danger of fun that is really lawlessness. I soon found out that they knew other boys who were
doing the same thing, but who had not been so fortunate as to be
caught. I did not let them tell me the names of the other boys.
I asked them to go to the boys and ask them if they would not
come to see me at my chambers and become my friends and
helpers and spare us all the disgrace of having the policemen on
their trail. The other boys soon got interested and were really
anxious to come. They want to be in the game, and then grad-
ually they all get together and then comes the "snitching bee."

By this we mean that every boy in the court around my table in chambers, when no one is there except the judge and the boys, tells on himself, and in telling on himself has permission from the other boys to tell the whole thing, including the names of those present who are "in it." What one forgets the other remembers, and they soon vie with each other as to who can tell the most and who has been the worst. This is in no spirit of boasting, however. The fact that I know personally, as Judge of the Juvenile Court, every one of those boys and every misdemeanor in which he has been engaged, ditching cars and everything else, puts the Judge in a powerful position with respect to the boys. Of course, they agree among themselves to stop the lawlessness, and everybody consents that the boys not only can but it shall be their duty to "snitch" (tell) on a boy who repeats the offense. This is done for the sake of the neighborhood, for the sake of the school. Every ennobling instinct of loyalty and pride (generally a predominant characteristic in boys) is brought to bear in behalf of law and order, and the result is that the trouble that was chronic and of long standing is broken up, and I have yet to know of a single case, after three years of work of this kind, where a boy was brought back for a second offense of the same kind. They have been loyal and faithful and the entire police force of Denver could not begin to have accomplished, by arrests and incarcerations, one-half that the boys themselves have accomplished in the suppression of this kind of rowdyism and lawlessness. All that is necessary is to catch two or three of the culprits, and if you understand the boys and the boys understand you the rest is not only easy but absolutely a joy. It is great fun both for the Judge and the boys. It is really more fun to "stop it" than it was to "do it."

HOW BOYS ENFORCE THE LAW.

In a certain suburb where the smelters are located and there are a great many cheap saloons selling bad liquor and tobacco to children, two celebrated gangs brought to the Juvenile Court for dangerous forms of rowdyism and lawlessness not only completely suppressed every serious, objectionable feature among themselves, but also got after the men who were selling liquor and tobacco to boys, prosecuted, and sent several to jail, and did more to stop the use of tobacco and liquor among boys in that neighborhood than the police department or civil authorities had done in the history of the town. In fact, the boys in the Juvenile Court of Denver, we can say without hesitation and without intending any reflection upon the civil authorities or police department, have prosecuted and convicted more men for selling liquor and tobacco to children, for selling them firearms, junk dealers for purchasing stolen property, men for circulating immoral literature, in one year of the Juvenile Court than the entire police department, sheriff's office and all other civil officers combined, have done in twenty years. It has all been done "on the square." The boys have been cautioned that they must never entrap anyone and they have never received a cent except the commendation of others and the satisfaction of having become "good little citizens." It is not an infrequent thing to have a boy come to my chambers and tell me that Mr. —— sold Johnny so and so cigarettes or liquor and he would like to file a complaint. Recently a little fellow of 12 came to me joyously and said: "Judge, old Mr. —— that runs the drug store on our corner, sells cigarettes, and Johnny B. went in there to get some and old Mr. —— got furious and said, 'You little rascal, get out of here just as quick as you can. How do I know that some of those kids out there don't belong to that Juvenile Court, and they will have me hauled up there to pay a hundred dollars for selling you a nickel's worth of tobacco. Get out of here and don't you ever come back again.' " Old Mr. ——'s discretion was as wise as his fears were well founded.

GET THE TRUTH.

Above all things get the truth. Never let a boy get away from you with a successful lie in his soul. You have lost the battle if you do. I have had several street boys tell me, after a struggle to get the truth, how "game" I was to win out. Most of them are conquered right there. Some officers, teachers and others will tell you most boys in delinquency lie. I could tell you the same thing in a way. As a rule it is not the boy's fault, and I do not consider him a liar. Often parents can not admit it is possible for the boy to be guilty of the offense. They are too willing to encourage his denials. There is pride to be mor-

tified if he is guilty. The preservation of the pride from mortification is too often more important than the preservation of
the boy's morals and the sensible view is not taken. Again,
there has not been companionship sufficient, or little confidences
have been neglected so that frankness and candor that always
yield the truth are likely to be absent or if present it may be in
dread of meeting a "licking" instead of sympathy, love and the
right kind of correction. But to get the truth go at a boy right,
allay his fears and the discords in his soul, make him see it is
to his interest to tell the truth, for he is entitled to be made to
see all this if we are fair. If we do this, I have found him the
most truthful creature in the world. Is not this rather the true
and fair test? Is not self-preservation the first law of nature?
Make it to his interest to tell the truth. If he is to get a "licking"
or expulsion from school for telling the truth, and if he is a
natural creature, he is mighty likely to lie. We need patience
and intelligence in dealing with such delicate matters.

LEGAL TECHNICALITIES AVOIDED BY THE JUVENILE COURT.

It will be observed that we pay very little attention to the
rules of evidence. The whole proceeding is in the interest of the
child and not to degrade him or even to punish him. We do not
protect the child by discharging him because there is no legal
evidence to convict as would be done in a criminal case when we
know that he has committed the offense. This is to do him a
great injury, for he is simply encouraged in a prevalent opinion
among city children, and adults also, for that matter, that it is
all right to lie all they can, to cheat all they can, to steal all they
can, so long as they "do not get caught," or that you have "no
proof." We make the boy understand that it is for his interest
to get caught if he has committed an error, and, unless demanded
(and it never has been in a single case out of about 2,000), we pay
absolutely no attention to the rules of evidence. We get the
truth and we are always sure we get the truth and nothing but
the truth.

WHERE THE CRIMINAL LAW FAILS.

Let me illustrate: Recently two boys from Capitol Hill, the
best residence district of Denver, according to the value of real

estate and the material magnificence of homes, were brought to me charged with stealing a watch. There was absolutely no evidence against them except suspicious circumstances, and, under a criminal proceeding, the case would have been dismissed and the boys found not guilty and returned home encouraged in the idea that they might do anything so long as there was no proof and they were not caught. I took those boys and their father to my chambers. He was a prominent business man, who protested their innocence, and, well meaning enough, encouraged their protestations and denials by his indignant denunciations of those who would cast suspicion upon his boys. The neighbors who had lost the watch also came to my chambers. Of course, the father was willing to find out the truth, as people usually are when you go at them right—that is, with tact and judgment. The result of one hour's earnest talk with those boys was that their lives for the first time were laid bare to their business father. They not only stole the watch, but practiced the most artful deception in covering it up and endeavored to lay the guilt upon another boy by secreting the watch in his pocket and subjecting him to suspicion and accusation. But they had stolen money from the same neighbors; they had stolen money from their own father time and again; they had played truant from school without his knowledge. They told "smutty stories;" they were addicted to profanity, cigarette smoking and about every vile thing that should not be in any wholesome boy's life. That father went away from the Court a sadder but a wiser man. It would be difficult to tell you how, without the slightest trouble, I got those boys to tell the truth, or how I was absoluely certain the moment I spoke to them that they had been lying to their father; that they had committed the offense of which they were only suspected. Those experienced and earnestly interested in such work soon become unusually proficient in distinguishing truth from falsehood and recognizing "ghost stories" and exaggeration (common in childhood) as distinguished from the real facts.

HOW THE TRUTH SAVED THE BOY.

I have in mind two interesting cases: One in which the father and mother of the boy were at first rather indignant at

A TYPE

my unhesitating statement that their boy was guilty of the offense charged where nothing but meagre and unsatisfactory circumstantial evidence developed. Their indignation was promptly allayed when they understood me, and I secured their permission, before dismissing the case, to spend fifteen minutes with the boy, on condition that no one but the boy, myself and his parents should know the result. I took the boy into my chambers and told him that he was not a liar, although he had testified under oath on the witness stand to what I knew was false. I told him he was a good boy, but I told him I despised his deception and he could never hope to be anything but a sneak if he did not "cut out" the vile things he had done and show me and his parents that he was what I said he was, and what I should tell them that he was, namely, a truthful boy and a good boy, by doing what I knew he would do when he rightly understood. I refused to let him say a word until I had finished. I then described to him his emotions and the things that made him lie because of his weakness. I told him how frightened he was at the prospect of being detected. I put my hand on his head and looked into his face and told him how I admired his love for his father and mother whom he did not want to give pain and mortification by admitting his offense, after he had so strenuously denied it, and then I explained and argued with him how, in the end, this was all a mistake and how once, when I was a boy, I had told a "whopping big lie" and had always regretted it, and could never have amounted to anything had I kept up such a course. When I finished the tears came into his eyes, he put out his hand and thanked me and told me how he had committed the theft and how deceitful he had been and how sorry he was, and how, with my help and kindness, he was going to overcome it. And when his mother and father came into my room I told them that they had a splendid boy who had only yielded to temptation once or twice in a moment of weakness, and whom I respected now more than I ever did before, because he had strength enough to see the right and do the right, and they should take him home, not to thrash him as was his father's first impulse after the shock and surprise were over, but rather to deal firmly with him by other methods than the rod and the anger I know was excited in the mind of his father, who was a firm and stern man, and who was angry more from wounded pride and mortification, more because of selfishness, than because of love for his boy.

I remember one other case of a blue-eyed, rather good-looking youngster who was called as a witness against another boy for stealing a bicycle. He was called by the man who lost the wheel. Almost thoughtlessly, and, perhaps, indiscreetly, as the boy sat on the witness stand, I turned to him and asked him to tell me how many times he himself had stolen. He expressed himself as very much surprised, and, of course, denied that he had ever stolen anything. His mother was with him, and was, naturally, perhaps justly indignant. I apologized and then I got the mother and the boy together, and when the mother saw my interest in him she gave me permission to talk with him, as she said, to disabuse my mind of such an unwarranted and preconceived idea. In just fifteen minutes Harry had admitted to me the theft of two bicycles, considerable money from his mother and one or two neighbors. He volunteered to go on probation and report to me regularly thereafter.

A CASE THAT ALMOST FAILED.

I never became provoked with but one boy out of hundreds with whom I have thus talked in my chambers and I was so satisfied that he was lying, although I had not one word of proof, that I sent for an officer and told him that he should take him to jail until he could make up his mind to tell the truth. I have, for certain reasons, always regretted this. He had not gone a block with the officer when he expressed a desire to return. He came up to my table and put out his hand and said: "Judge, that is the 'gamiest' fight I ever had, and you have 'won out.' I lied like a horse-thief. I hope you will forgive me." This boy was one of the toughest specimens ever brought to us by the police department and I was interested in the fight. I remember, in the course of our talk, I told him that from certain things, Sherlock Holmes would have made certain deductions. I had interested this boy in reading Dr. Doyle's detective stories because when I first got hold of him he had confided to me his ambition to be a second "Tracy, the Outlaw." I hoped he might in the end change his ambition and become a good detective, and he replied to my deductions that if I thought any such thing that Sher-

6

lock Holmes was a bum detective. After I had won the "gamiest fight he ever had," he added: "And I will tell you, Judge, I want to apologize to Sherlock Holmes." Among other things this boy had lied to me about his knowledge of the whereabouts of another dangerous character among the street boys. I had occasion subsequently to ask him a similar question and he promptly replied that he knew where the boy was but felt that it would be wrong to tell. Whereupon I promptly agreed with him. In forty-eight hours, and about 10 o'clock at night, he brought this boy to my house, and as the boy was a fugitive from justice under a sentence to the State Reformatory, he said that he had made up his mind that I was so blanked "square" that he was ready to take his papers and go to Buena Vista (where the Reformatory is located). Of course, I had not the heart to take up the proposition, and the young fellow is now working in the city of Denver.

Such are some of the results of the struggle for truth.

TROUBLES OF CHILDREN.

Few people have any conception of the number of children who come voluntarily to the Juvenile Court for help, both moral and financial. Recently a certain little Sam, aged 12, who sells papers and attends the newsboys' meetings in the old court room, came to me one evening to say that his mother could not do anything with his little brother of 10, and he wanted me to help. Sam is a manly little fellow and it is half pitiful and half amusing to observe that mixture of maturity and childishness expressed in his talk to me. He was as near a father as he could be at the age of 12. I told him to send Willie up at 5 the next day, and promptly at 5 o'clock Willie came, saying that he had never seen me before but had heard of me. He came all alone. He looked rather sheepish, and it was not long before he told me all of his misdemeanors and promised to come and see me once a week until he could be really good and "cut out" all of the bad things he had been doing down in the street. Sam now reports that Willie is all right.

NOT AFRAID TO BE CAUGHT.

One day, at the close of a busy session of the civil court, I noticed a little fellow sitting back in the court room all alone.

I called him up to the bench. I had never seen him before. His reticence at first was the result rather of shyness than of fear, and, with tears in his eyes, he told me that he was 10 years old, that his father had deserted his mother, and that his mother had gone away and left him; that he was living with a good lady and that he had been "swiping" things for a long time, and some of the kids had told him if he kept it up the "cop" would get him and he had better come and tell me all about it, and I would get him out of trouble, and help to make him good. This little Clifford was placed on probation. He brings good reports, and it seems to delight him immensely when I tell the group of boys as he comes up to hand in his report, how he was not afraid to get caught and how he has "cut it out."

HOW THE BOYS REGARD THE COURT.

Only last week we found the following among the troubles of children: Johnny G., who works as bell boy at a private hotel, spilled some ink upon the floor. His employer deducted ten dollars from his pay. He had no money to employ a lawyer, and but for his confidence in the power of the Court, fear of losing his position would have sealed his lips. He came and told his troubles freely and it will be settled fairly and justly and he will not lose his place. Another working boy has complained of damage to his wheel. It will be investigated and if justice is upon his side he will get justice. Only recently a poor boy came to see me, complaining that a man came and took away his wheel, claiming it had been stolen. The probation officer was immediately dispatched to investigate the case, with the result that the man returned the wheel and apologized to the boy because he had made a mistake. A glance at the monthly reports of the probation officers will show the enormous amount of work of this kind done, all of which tends to make these children respecters of the law, and teaches them to look upon the State as their friend and protector and the Juvenile Court as a place where justice is truly meted out, and everything that is done is for and not against them.

EMPLOYMENT BUREAU.

A glance at the probation officer's report will also show the enormous amount of work that is necessary to help city boys obtain employment of the right kind. As shown before we make no distinction between boys who have been in court and those who have not been in court, so that it is so well known that because boys come around the Juvenile Court it is no sign of wrong-doing that it relieves the place of any stigma or odium which might otherwise attach if a different spirit were fostered in the work.

VISITATION BY PROBATION OFFICERS.

We believe that paid probation officers, because of the very fact that it is their duty, can visit homes where necessary, with much better effect than voluntary probation officers, especially where such officers lack the tact and judgment necessary in such cases. Upon the skill, tact, and diplomacy of such officer, depends much of the success of the Court. A voluntary officer is sometimes looked upon as an intermeddler and not received with the consideration which the office should command. We have no voluntary probation officers in the Juvenile Court of Denver, although, from time to time, in exceptional cases, the intervention of several of our friends has been of special value. The services of a wise, discreet and tactful probation officer are of inestimable value.

PARENTS' MEETINGS.

Parents of the boys are frequently consulted by the probation officers, and if it meets with general approval, it is proposed during the next two years to have meetings of the parents of all boys reporting to the Court in order that harmony and co-operation between the Court and the home may be promoted.

SCHOOL PRINCIPALS' MEETINGS.

At the close of the last school year the principals of all the schools in Denver were invited to a meeting at the Juvenile Court to discuss the Juvenile work from the standpoint of the schools, in order that we might receive suggestions for the improvement of the work and any friendly criticism as to where it was weak, the officers of the Court feeling that there were a number of weak spots because of lack of help and facilities and as perfect co-operation as could be wished in several particulars. Some thirty principals attended and all expressed themselves as being more than satisfied with the progress of the work, and, though freely invited, no criticisms were offered. The school attendance officers, the school teachers, principals and superintendents are acting in perfect harmony and co-operation with the Court. The Court is only too glad to have the principals and school authorities speak freely of any mistakes they observe, and every effort will be made to correct them. The officers of the Juvenile Court do not consider the system as by any means perfect, or even as satisfactory as they could wish and intend it shall be, so far as it lies in their power, with the facilities and machinery provided. It is the desire of the Court during the coming school year, to have an occasional meeting of the principals and teachers of all those schools having probationers, in order that the best methods may be considered, and co-operation and harmony between the two departments promoted and continued as in the past.

INCREASE IN JUVENILE DELINQUENCY.

The first few years at least of any Juvenile Court is almost certain to show a marked increase in the number of children apprehended. There are two principal causes for this: First, people in various neighborhoods who are the victims in property or person of lawlessness, or organized gangs, in the old days found it generally useless to appeal to the police authorities, because those authorities were almost as helpless as they. If the culprits were arrested the police department could only put them in jail or subject them to some treatment, the tendency of which was of doubtful value, or allow them to go without restraint beyond a reprimand, which sometimes was an indication of weakness that often encouraged rather than discouraged such lawlessness. So serious cases were often allowed to go without restraint or attempted correction. It being now generally known that there is a forum better equipped for handling such cases, not only are the serious cases brought to the Court, but there is a disposition on the part of a great many people to rush to the Juvenile Court with children's troubles that are really trifling and should not be dignified with notice by the officers of the Court. It is sometimes hard to draw distinctions. To avoid this as far as possible, the probation officer carefully investigates complaints made and settles many cases in the homes with the parents, with the result that the complaining victims of such lawlessness are spared the mortification of a more formal proceeding, and saved the expense of filing court cases and the trial thereof.

CHILDREN BETTER CARED FOR.

A second reason for an increase in such cases, as already indicated, is the fact that both dependent and delinquent children are better looked after, cared for and protected and corrected because of the interest of the officers and the machinery provided.

HOW THE CASE GROWS.

I have a rather interesting and actual illustration of this in the case of two boys caught in the dry goods stores downtown stealing small trinkets. These two boys were brought to the Judge's chambers by the officer apprehending them. By getting them interested they confessed all of their misdemeanors and, in answer to my question, assured me they knew of other boys doing the same thing.

THE SNITCHING BEE.

In the "snitching bee" (to "snitch" is to tell), conducted in my chambers around my table, after the boys became friendly, they did not tell the names of the boys they knew to be doing the same thing, but they went back to the school and within the next day or so returned to my chambers with sixteen more. These sixteen boys, from a very respectable school in a respectable neighborhood, returned to me some twenty or thirty dollars' worth of stolen trinkets, principally agate marbles, leather purses and bags, which they use for carrying their marbles. They voluntarily joined the delinquent list of probationers. Every single boy who was "in it" was thus brought to the Juvenile Court, whereas, under the criminal law only the two who were caught would have suffered the penalty and the remainder would have been encouraged not to get caught, without the more important lesson to fear to do wrong. But this was not all.

HOW THE DRAGNET WORKS.

As everybody was anxious to tell all their misdemeanors, we undertook to find out as far as we could the causes of the troubles, and, in the case of every boy, to correct as far as we could any shortcoming in his environment which might tend to his degradation; so every boy who had been in the saloons or bought cigarettes was called upon to tell about it, not in any boasting way, but in order "never to do it again." And those who had sent them to the saloons and the men who had furnished them the liquor or tobacco were found out. The result was that several mothers and fathers were added to the list; and so the case which started in the Juvenile Court with two little culprits and would have there ended in the criminal court, jumped from two to twenty-two men, women and children. Their faults were corrected and not one of these boys has ever been committed, because they have given up their bad habits under the influence and direction of the Court, aided by the enforced responsibility of the parents.

Another most interesting case of this character was one where the party caught numbered four and these four rounded up forty-four others. In another case the party caught numbered six or seven and these rounded up fifty-two others. It has been about two years since any one of these happenings, and in none of the cases so far has there been either a complaint against any one of the boys involved or any other boys in the same neighborhood because of a repetition of the offense. Surely, therefore, the increase in numbers brought to the Juvenile Court, under a system like this, would be no indication of an increase of juvenile lawlessness or juvenile depravity, but, on the contrary, the healthiest possible sign of the fact that it was being better handled and better coped with, with the assurance of an ultimate decrease of such offenses.

A POSITIVE DECREASE IN JUVENILE OFFENSES IN DENVER.

It has been the occasion of frequent remark among all the officers connected with the Juvenile Court that we do not begin to have the number of cases, and certainly not such serious cases of theft and burglary and stealing from the railroads as were very common in the early history of this Court. Mrs. Clark, the efficient matron of the city jail, recently told the writer that even before the house of detention was started the falling off in the numbers of boys brought to her department was extremely marked and the occasion of frequent comment. The special officers detailed by the railroad companies and the dry goods stores have voluntarily complimented the Court upon the remarkable decrease in cases handled by them. The general manager of one of the largest railroads in the State told the writer recently that since the Juvenile Court was inaugurated they had been able to ·dispense with one of the men employed to protect their property from juvenile lawlessness, because of the amazing decrease, and all of these officers have expressed the opinion that 90 per cent. is an average and conservative estimate of such decrease.

TRUANCY DECREASING.

Truancy is certainly by no means as alarming and prevalent as it was formerly. We invite the attention of the reader to a few of the letters published in the chapter on "The Court Approved," both as to the decrease in juvenile offenses in Denver and the saving of expense to the State. Considering the natural reasons, because of the different handling, for the increase in numbers brought to the Juvenile Court, the results so far are all the more encouraging.

TRUST AND CONFIDENCE IN BOYS.

Considerable has already been said respecting the methods of this Court in placing trust and confidence in the boys. This has been carried to the rather unusual extent of sending boys to the detention school with their own orders of detention. I have had some of the worst boys taken from their cells in the jail and brought to my chambers by careful officers who expected them to attempt to escape. I have never hesitated in the worst of such cases, after I have had a talk with the boy and was satisfied that I understood him and he understood me, to return them to the jail alone and unattended through the crowded city. Not a single boy returned by me to the jail alone has ever failed to promptly report and take his place behind the bars.

BOYS GO TO JAIL AND INDUSTRIAL SCHOOL ALONE.

We have now committed eighteen boys to the Industrial School at Golden, who have taken their own warrants of com mitment, taken the electric cars in Denver alone, gone through the crowded city, changed cars down among the railroad tracks, with every opportunity to escape, and without the knowledge of the officers at the Industrial School that they were coming, left the train at the Industrial School station near the foothills, and have gone straight to the superintendent's office and there delivered themselves and made return upon their writs. This plan was looked upon with doubt and suspicion, not only by the police, but by some of the best friends and officers of the Court. Not one has failed to do all that he promised and all that was expected.

WHO THE BOYS ARE.

These boys are of every type from the little chronic runaway of 11 or 12, pursued and hunted by the police and brought screaming to my chambers in charge of an officer in full uniform, to boy burglars of 16, who have been transferred from one jail to another shackled and placed in close confinement.

IF WE SHOULD FAIL.

Of course, I may some day be disappointed. I am looking forward to that day with a great deal of interest in order to find out why the boy would not go, for I shall have something interesting to learn and can only be the better for such an experience rather than the worse, for we have never lost a boy yet, and should such a case arise, when the boy is retaken we will almost certainly start him out again.

THE PURPOSE OF THE PLAN.

There is an important purpose in this plan. I have found from talking with a great many boys in Industrial Schools that they felt they were the victims of force and violence; they did not look upon the State as their friend, but as their enemy, and when they came out it was often with ill will and hatred towards some one connected with the State. By the plan we pursue the boy is made to feel that he and he alone is responsible for his condition. He knows he has had a fair show and a square deal, and when he comes out of the school he is perfectly free to come back to our Court, knowing that he will be welcome and helped and assisted. I try to visit the Industrial School as frequently as possible and I feel that I can justly say that every boy in that institution is my friend and cherishes no feeling of resentment towards me. On the contrary, I have a great many devoted correspondents among the boys, and every indication of the warmest regard and affection. In fact, the correspondence with boys in a great many states whose friendship is so lasting as not to be out of mind when out of sight, is becoming so large that it is a large item of the juvenile work. In my recent trip to the Pacific coast, in every one of the cities of the four or five states I visited, one of the first in to see me was some boy who had been to the Juvenile Court of Denver.

NEEDY CHILDREN RELIEVED.

We have found it very helpful for the best work among some of the delinquent boys in this Court to provide a fund for their relief. During the winter months especially children frequently come to the Court poorly shod and clad. Through the kindness of some of the ladies in furnishing clothing, and a number of citizens in making small donations, the Court has maintained a fairly respectable relief fund, which has been administered as judiciously and wisely as possible. Many such cases may properly be sent to the Charity Association, which has always shown the friendliest disposition to help us, and yet at the same time such cases are sometimes so urgent that we find it more satisfactory to render relief from the probation office.

A CASE IN POINT.

I remember getting off the train coming into Denver one cold morning when a poorly shod little boy came up to the passengers through the depot to carry their baggage. I stopped the boy and asked him if he did not know he would get into the Juvenile Court for being out of school. He said he was too sharp for the Juvenile Court, and that Judge Lindsey could never catch him. He insisted that he had a right to "smash baggage" if he could make a quarter, as he needed it to help his mother. I took the boy with me to the court house, against his cries and protestations. He was shod and decently clad, placed upon probation, and through the assistance rendered the home and the boy, he has become one of our warmest supporters and one of the best boys in the Court. Of course, he had "swiped things."

The father of several boys reporting to the Court was sentenced to jail for six months for participating in a labor riot at the smelters. The financial assistance rendered these boys and the work obtained for them did more to prevent their return to delinquent habits than the moral suasion we might have brought to bear.

Last Christmas, through the donations of the merchants of Denver and many friends of the Court, an elaborate Christmas entertainment was planned for the boys in the Juvenile Court room. Every boy on the probation list who desired to come was invited. The Christmas presents consisted of good things in the way of fruits, nuts, games and books, and every boy was given 50 cents in money. We can truly say that there was no happier crowd of children in Denver than these boys, over half of whom were from the poorest homes and neighborhoods in the city. Their behavior was commented on by a number of persons as being even better than that of children at some of the Sunday school Christmas trees among the children of the financially well-to-do.

LACK OF NOURISHMENT.

The lack of physical nourishment, proper food, cleanliness, wholesome sanitary conditions and sufficient clothing is not only responsible for a great deal of unhappiness and suffering among children, but directly contributes to their delinquency. The children of the best homes would be no different if subjected to the same conditions. We, therefore, feel that if we expect the child to reform it is only just and fair to improve such conditions as far as we can. I have visited the tenements and homes of the children of the poor in our largest cities, and while we have no such general surroundings or slum conditions as we have there, yet the two most miserable homes into which I have ever entered I found right here in Denver. The dirt upon the floors was actually deep enough to plant seed in; the bed clothing was grimy and filthy, and vermin more plentiful in the children's heads than anywhere else, while the atmosphere was fairly reeking. In both of these cases material assistance has been rendered. In one of these homes there are two really handsome boys. The father deserted and gone, no one knows where; the mother soured, cynical and melancholy, slaving all day as a scrub woman, and living, practically, in a hell on earth. Is it strange that these boys do not stay at home nights and are attracted by the bright lights and music of the cheap theaters and dance halls? Is it strange that they will steal money to enter such places, which are, to them, heaven come to earth? I have known such little fellows to lie in jail for days and days awaiting trial for small thefts. How blindly absurd and ridiculous it all seems that nothing was done to remove the causes that were making criminals for the State until they should be sentenced to jail, which only added to the misery and absurdity of the situation; for it is such boys that I have known to be in jail time and time again, while the State slept on, believing that it was doing its duty to society, that it was protecting society, when it was merely adding itself to the seething mass that is yielding up the criminals of the future.

THE FIGHT AGAINST THE JAIL.

The jail was not abolished without work and a fight. When the fight was on a police commissioner said the boys lied to me about the corruption in the jail. I sent for the Governor of the State, the Mayor of Denver, the District Attorney and the president of the council, the police board and a dozen ministers of the gospel to listen to the story that the boys and I could tell them. They came. I sent "Mickey" to the street for the boys and for three hours they heard a story of filth and depravity from boys 9 to 15 years of age that was so horrible and revolting that it did seem hard to believe, yet it was so true that the Governor rose up and declared that anyone who said the boys lied, lied himself. The ministers preached on it, and in three days our bill was passed, signed by Governor Peabody, and the jail for little children in Denver was down and out forever. Thousands of our boys had been locked up there all day and all night entirely alone. What happened can be imagined, but they never told, because no one cared. No one knew the facts. It was not the management so much as the system itself that was all wrong.

The State will never make progress in this far-reaching problem until it abolishes the method of the jail and the criminal court, with their foul spirits of punishment and revenge, and establishes in lieu thereof a system that will implant in wayward children lessons of purity, truth, honor, righteousness and industry, so that there may be a soul-awakening instead of a soul-debasing.

THE TRUE FUNCTION OF THE JUVENILE COURT.

Much has already been said and written here and by others concerning the true function of the Juvenile Court. Yet I desire to make some observations from my own experience and a careful study of criminality and its causes for several years past.

This Court should be regarded rather in the light of a school than a court. It should be one great moral improvement association. Its chief members and workers should be those who need the improvement, just as men band together in societies to improve themselves along different lines. Because of the relation of the State to crime and the judicial system built up in this country for the correction and punishment of crime, it may be impossible as well as undesirable to eliminate the court from the machinery necessary to carry out the real principle and purpose back of what has been termed the Juvenile Court and probation system.

THE JUDGE OF THE JUVENILE COURT.

And yet, if this were not so, I should say it was just as absurd to require the ordinary judge to preside over a Juvenile Court as it would be to require him to superintend and manage a State Industrial School or a Sunday school. Ordinarily, judges are not fitted by training or disposition to preside in such courts; neither could they be expected to enter into what seems to me the true duties of a judge of a Juvenile Court. It is proper, therefore, that most of the personal work should be done under the system as it now stands, by the probation officers; yet the influence of the judge, where he can take a personal interest in such cases, is an important factor in the good that can be accomplished. There are a number of judges in several cities who have shown to a remarkable extent this personal interest, and the success of the Court is largely due to them; yet there are other cases where, because of the enormous amount of work more properly of a judicial character, even should there be no lack of disposition to enter into the spirit of the juvenile work, it can neither be done nor rightly expected. I think the Court should be a great leavening power for good in the community in every direction it can justly and properly go. Of course, what can be done must depend largely upon the jurisdiction, the particular city and its own peculiar conditions.

THE WORK IMPORTANT.

I regard the work of the juvenile division of the Court as the most important work it can be called upon to administer. Surely every case involving a boy or a girl is more important than any case involving dollars and cents, no matter what the amount may be. The proper rearing and handling of children in the home, the church, and in so far as the Juvenile Court is called in to help, will do more than any other one thing, not only to reduce criminal proceedings in court, but also civil proceedings. It is, nearer than any one thing, the foundation of all of these problems. We must, therefore, awaken to its importance and spare neither earnest work nor money in caring for the children of the State. We must proceed on the thory that we cannot best overcome the waywardness of children by punishment and force. We must overcome falsehood with truth, dishonor with honor, impurity with purity, unrighteousness with righteousness, evil with good. This is, and must continue to be, the doctrine of the Juvenile Court. There must be love at the foundation of it all, and with this there must be justice. Love without justice may become sentimentality and weakness, but there is no justice without love. The State in the past has not done this, and no one has suffered more than the State and the society it stands for, and it will continue to suffer just in proportion as it forgets that all men are brothers and all boys and girls its children and that they deserve to be treated accordingly. It is only in this way that we shall come nearer to the teachings of our Lord and Master, and none but the ignorant or brutal or those looking for the easiest method can mistake this doctrine for leniency or weakness, for it is as far removed from the maudlins of the sentimentalist as is the heartless advocate of vengeance or "an eye for an eye and a tooth for a tooth." The torture chamber, the inquisition and even death for trivial offenses, have passed from our civilization forever, and the entire Juvenile Court system is simply another evidence that should fill us with hope, for it faces the dawn.

JUVENILE COURT ONLY A PART OF THE SYSTEM.

Of course, the Juvenile Court is only one of a great many things that are combining to bring about the change; no one could well accomplish it alone. Perhaps all could not accomplish it entirely. The great work of the children's aid and home finding societies, the orphans' homes, the industrial schools and occasionally a great man like John L. Whitman of the Cook County jail have their places in the work of reform.

DO NOT EXPECT TOO MUCH. TEST OF SUCCESS.

Too much must not be expected of the Juvenile Court; it is not necessary to claim it. It is a success, even conceding all of its mistakes and failures, if it is only better than the old method. Every one must admit this. And even if the administrative work is not done as it should be, it is better to have juvenile laws if the only effect be the single change of permitting the correction of children without stigmatizing them with crime upon the threshold of life. There is really no argument against the juvenile law, nor the spirit and purpose back of it. There may be occasion for just criticism of those who administer it, but this must not be confounded with criticism or objection to the law itself. Because judges may inflict slight penalties or no penalties at all in criminal cases would not be considered by some critics of the juvenile law as a reason for abolishing the laws against criminality.

THE JUVENILE IMPROVEMENT ASSOCIATION.

As an auxiliary to the work of the Juvenile Court, a number of our best citizens have formed the Juvenile Improvement Association of Denver. The purpose of this organization is to encourage social betterment for children. The plan was proposed about a year ago and has met with much favor.

1 EARLY MORNING   BEET FIELD CAMP   2 AT WORK

WORK IN THE BEET FIELDS.

Among the things which the society proposes is to take advantage of the opportunity in the northern and southern sugar beet fields to supply city boys with work during the summer. Average boys will not work in school unless the teacher is present; neither are they likely to work in the fields unless some capable person is there to encourage and direct them. It is not surprising, therefore, that boys heretofore sent to the beet fields without organization or discipline did not give general satisfaction. It is now proposed to send a probation officer in charge of each twenty boys, with a complete camp outfit, which is to be pitched in the most favorable place near the fields. A number of such camps have been organized, and at the present writing are being sent to the fields, with every prospect of success. These boys have been meeting faithfully with the judge and the probation officers in the Juvenile Court upon designated evenings, when their work and its importance, not only to the farmers but to themselves, to the Court and to the Improvement Association, is freely discussed. The boys are thus made to feel their responsibility, and while we cannot tell what success may be had or what we can do until we try, we are looking forward with much interest to the result of this plan. Last year something over one hundred boys were sent to the beet fields from Denver. They were allowed to do very much as they pleased, and with the same results as would happen in any well regulated school of the best boys. Less than one-half of them gave satisfaction. Yet something over twenty families went from the slums to the beet fields because of the experiment, and notwithstanding its disappointments, we account it to have been more than worth while.

The Court is under great obligations to Mrs. J. J. Brown and her able assistants, Mrs. Margaret Fealy, Mrs. Alexander Helme and the young ladies who assisted them in the entertainment given at the Broadway Theater in April, 1904, for raising funds for this Association and the promotion of the beet field work. The beet sugar industry in Colorado is assuming enormous proportions and demands a class of work in the fields for three months in the summer—June to September, vacation months— which can be well performed by boys under proper discipline. We are simply trying to avail ourselves of these opportunities for the good of the boys.

1 Ready for the Day's Work   2 Resting

WORK IN THE BEET FIELD

SUCCESS IN THE BEET FIELDS.

Greeley, Colo., June 30, 1904.

Hon. Ben B. Lindsey,
          Denver, Colorado,

Dear Sir:—

I have had for the past ten days in my employ eleven of your boys under charge of Officer Withers, at work thinning beets at the Lucerne ranch at Peckham, Colorado. I have also had employed a gang of Mexicans and a gang of Japanese, working in the same field, and I wish to tell you that the boys have done the best work of all of them in that field. Their work has been done better and they have caused less trouble than any other beet thinners I have had in my employ for the last three years.

I write to tell you that I am satisfied with their work and that the boys are deserving of all the praise that I can give them. If another season you desire to send out boys to thin beets, please bear me in mind, as I would rather have them than any other help.

Yours truly,

P. W. ALLEN.

———————

La Salle, Colo., July 3, 1904.

Hon. Ben. B. Lindsey,
          Juvenile Court, Denver, Colo.

Dear Sir:—

Yours of the 30th at hand and am pleased to answer same. The work done by the boys has been very satisfactory.

I do not see any reason why these boys cannot be made self-supporting, and most of them good citizens, instead of a city nuisance. Boys are better adapted to this work than older people, and under good management there is no reason why they cannot do better work and do it easier.

Very truly yours,

R. M. BARR,
Assistant Agricultural Superintendent Greeley Sugar Co.

Brush, Colo., July 6, 1904.

Hon. Ben. B. Lindsey,
    Juvenile Court, Denver, Colo.

Dear Sir:—

In reply to your letter of recent date I will say that the boys have blocked and thinned my beets in a good manner, and I think they did well, considering their experience, as mine was the first job they had. With proper management I believe the boys can be trained to do good work in blocking and thinning.

Yours truly,

D. W. McSWEEN,
Chairman Board County Commissioners.

———————————

Greeley, Colo., July 6, 1904.

Hon. Ben. B. Lindsey,
    Juvenile Court, Denver, Colo.

Dear Sir:—

We are in receipt of yours of June 30th, in which you asked us to give a statement in regard to the worth of the boy in the beet field.

In answer will say that the boys did well. They were a little unfortunate in the first field, as they had the hardest beets to thin there were in the district, but they thinned them, and did a good job. The other fields were all right and I understand they did fairly well. I visited the camp often and always found the boys in good humor and always willing to do what the officer told them.

Very truly yours,

H. TIMOTHY,
Agricultural Superintendent Greeley Sugar Co.

BOYS' CLUBS.

This association is also at the present time engineering three or four boys' clubs in those parts of the city where they are most needed. In such neighborhoods it has supplied baseball suits for baseball nines, and exacts in return the promise of the boys in that neighborhood to enforce the law. Some of this work is largely experimental, but so far gives promise of eminent justification. If conducted along intelligent and practical lines there can be no more important civic work than that intended for the moral betterment of the city's youth.

RECOMMENDATIONS AS PREVENTATIVES OF DELINQUENCY.

To this end a number of recommendations were made in the last annual report of the Juvenile Court, and will be here repeated, with such additions as have occurred to us during the past year.

USE OF SCHOOLS.

1st. We ask for more use of the school houses in those districts where it is most needed. Shower baths and club rooms could be justly provided. As we struggle with the Boys' Club down at the Railroad Mission and try to raise the funds for a shower bath, I think of the big school house off in the darkness, with its light and heat and janitor service going to waste and the boys who must go into that school attending this club and begging for these facilities. I have seen many of these boys around the saloons in the evenings and in the cheap theaters. We earnestly recommended the use of the schools for this purpose over a year ago, and trust the school board may feel justified in an experiment along this line. It has been done in other cities, and I have seen it in operation with great success.

UNGRADED ROOMS. INDUSTRIAL WORK.

2nd. We need ungraded rooms in a number of the schools, and, in my judgment, more manual and industrial work. I know that this will largely reduce delinquency and truancy in certain neighborhoods, because I have observed it in successful operation in other cities. The chapter herein upon the enormous expense to the State of delinquent children will show how absolutely economical every dollar spent for these improvements must in the end be to the State. Boys have no opportunity at this time to learn a trade in Colorado until they commit a crime, when they may be sent to the State Industrial School, where only a limited chance of this kind is given.

PLAY GROUNDS.

3rd. We earnestly recommend a few small parks or play grounds in crowded districts in several parts of the city. We could point these out to the park commission.

PARENTS' MEETINGS.

4th. Frequent parents' meetings in the schools, especially in those neighborhoods where environment is bad and the people are poor. Parents, whether rich or poor, can stand a good deal of education along the line of their duties and responsibilities towards their children. They should do the work, but in too many cases they can not or will not.

DETENTION SCHOOL.

5th. The Detention School has already proved so successful that a permanent institution of this kind should be built by the city.

JUVENILE BETTERMENT.

6th. The encouragement of every rational boys' club or plan for juvenile betterment proposed by responsible people, with the view of keeping children out of the Juvenile Court, as one of the longest steps towards the success of the real purpose of the Juvenile Court system.

ENFORCE LAWS.

7th. A rigid enforcement of those laws holding parents and others responsible for the delinquency of children in order to compel or assist the home and parents to perform their functions and thus relieve the State of taking their place. The institution is necessary and performs good work, but at best it can only be accounted a necessary evil where it has to supplant the home. The principal purpose of the probation system is to keep the child in the home and keep it out of institutions. No institution is better than a home. It is better than thousands of miserable places of habitation for children, mistakenly called homes. The best institutions are those nearest like the ideal home.

SCHOOL ATTENDANCE.

8th. A continued rigid enforcement of the compulsory edu-cation law as the best means of preventing truancy, which leads to deception, disobedience, idleness and crime. The best economy the school boards can practice in the end is the money it now spends in the compulsory education department for its superin-tendent and school attendance officers. I have no hesitancy in saying that even ten thousand dollars a year spent for five years in Denver for this purpose will save the city and State easily a million dollars in the course of twenty years, to say nothing of the moral addition to good citizenship.

CO-OPERATION.

9th. Continued close co-operation and harmonious work be-tween the schools and the Court.

POLICE DEPARTMENT.

10th. Closer co-operation and a better understanding be-tween the police department and the sheriff's office and the Juve-nile Court. I am delighted to say that there is already abundant evidence in these departments of greater satisfaction all round in this respect. The police department has been greatly handi-capped for lack of help, which we understand has necessitated a practice we are strongly opposed to, viz.: that of arresting chil-dren and detaining them at the city hall until the probation officer can remove them to the Detention School. An officer ar-resting a child should bring it immediately to the probation of-fice or the Detention School. It should not be taken to the city hall at all, notwithstanding the greatly improved arrangements

there and the excellent care given the children by the splendid
matrons in charge. The purpose of the new law was to keep
children away from any connection with the jail itself, and
however commendatory may be the additional precautions, it
does not fully comply with the requirements and spirit of the
law.

WORK BY TEACHERS.

11th. Special and particular interest by school teachers in
delinquent boys instead of that disposition often manifested to
get rid of them as a nuisance and as engendering extra work.
This must not be understood as indicating that there has been
a lack of proper disposition in this regard in Denver with reference to such cases. On the contrary, the school teachers of Denver are entitled to the warmest praise and commendation, as already declared in this report, for their cordial co-operation and
earnest work in this respect.

RECORDS AND ASSISTANCE.

12th. Owing to the greater care given to the children of
Denver under the new laws and the elaborate records we are undertaking and the extra work necessarily incurred with the new
system, we should have at least one more assistant for clerical
help and probation work. No one can appreciate the amount of
detail work that is constantly being done by the probation office
without a visit to, and personal inspection of, that office. This
work is one that has been absolutely neglected in communities
heretofore, but is now being regarded as of sufficient importance
in some cities to incur the expense of a separate exclusive court
with a special judge, clerical force, paid probation officers and
Detention House. During the past two years the County Court,
which is, in this State, the Juvenile Court, has performed all of
this work and turned over to the county over ten thousand dollars in cash as its earnings from litigants paying fees to the
Court under our fee system, after paying the salaries of the
judge and all the clerks. This surplus has been sufficient to
more than pay all of the expense of probation work, even since
those offices have been placed upon a salary, and considering the
enormous saving in money and morals as shown by the chapter

herein on expense, and considering the hundreds of thousands invested in this city in jails and the tens of thousands paid in salaries to prosecuting officers, sheriffs and policemen, all to detect and punish crime, it would be hard to understand the mental caliber or fathom the motive of the man who would object to any and every reasonable expense designed to save children and prevent crime.

MUTUAL HELPFULNESS.

13th. The encouragement of a fraternal and helpful spirit between all of those offices and others who have any part in this noble work. Let there be no jealousy, no "knocking" and no complaint until they have been first made to those who may be or should be responsible and every opportunity given to correct faults, mistakes and errors. No greater calamity could befall the work of the Juvenile Court than the discord which is the sure result of petty spites, petty selfishness, petty jealousies and petty complaints and fault-finding. Let the work be the thing, unselfishly and earnestly, into which goes the whole heart and soul.

THOSE WHO HAVE HELPED.

The most hopeful, helpful and encouraging thing about the Juvenile Court work of Denver has been a general spirit of approval thereof pervading the entire community. This very spirit, as it were, has been more responsible for the good accomplished than any individual or set of individuals engaged therein. It has indeed been fortunate, and it can only be the hope of the officers of this Court that it has been justly and fairly earned. Their gratefulness and appreciation and the humility and thankfulness it has inspired in those upon whom the direct burdens of this work devolve, and the inspiration it has been for resolves for the future, can never be fully known or understood except by those directly affected. It too often happens that the withholding of public support from a movement for civic betterment or reform, however worthy, is rather the cause of its failure than any lack of sincerity, earnestness or unselfishness on the part of those behind it.

Particularly the good women of Denver, the Women's Club, the mothers, the W. C. T. U., the churches, the press, the school authorities, the business men, the laboring people, and, in fact, all of the people, seem to have approved of the Juvenile Court in our midst and its power for usefulness and good. The Denver Tramway Company and the railroads have not only approved, but have encouraged and assisted the Court in many ways.

Outside of the officers composing the Court, the Humane Society has probably rendered the most assistance, through the efforts of its able secretary, Mr. E. K. Whitehead.

Special commendation is due the District Attorney's office, which has granted every request of the Court that might bring about a better enforcement of the law. The cases against parents and others offending have been wisely, tactfully and ably handled by Mr. Marcus A. Haines, deputy and assistant of Hon. H. A. Lindsley, the present District Attorney.

We have also to thank Mrs. Izetta George, secretary of the Associated Charity organization; also Hon. A. Newton Patton, chairman of the committee on charities of the city council, for uniform courtesy and ready assistance, especially for poor children and those mentally defective and requiring care in a home for their special benefit.

Hon. R. R. Wright, Jr., mayor of the city of Denver, without hesitation, appointed the superintendent and matron of the Detention School requested by the Court, and in these days of politics thereby showed a spirit as commendable as it is rare.

To Mr. Alexander Nesbit, the commissioner of supplies, and the city council are especially due the thanks of the Court for their assistance in establishing the Detention School. Dr. S. D. Hopkins has volunteered to take charge of the physical department and his work is greatly appreciated. Dr. C. B. James has also rendered valuable assistance.

It would be impossible, in this already lengthy report, and possibly in some instances distasteful to the individuals themselves, to mention all of their names. The generous approval here referred to is rather significant of that tenderness and nobility of heart that goes out to the misfortunes of children. It is this, rather than any commendation to which the Court may be entitled, that provokes so generous a response, and it is all the more gratifying that it is so, for it is the children's cause, and not any man or individual, that is deserving or entitled to such praise.

The Juvenile Court laws of Colorado were prepared by the judge of the Juvenile Court of Denver, assisted by the County Judges' Association, and were introduced in the Senate by Hon. Fred W. Bailey of Denver, and in the House by Hon. George W. Whyte of Leadville, assisted in the Senate largely by Hon. C. B. Ward of Boulder and Hon. Cyrus W. Dolph of Colorado Springs. Hon. Jesse R. Moler, Representative from Denver, introduced the present child labor law. The enactment of these bills into laws was made certain through the efforts of these gentlemen, with Hon. James H. Peabody, Governor of Colorado, who aided and assisted in the passage of the laws. They are entitled to the everlasting gratitude of the people of this State.

WHY HELP IS NEEDED IN THE COURT.

The county court of Denver is one of the busiest civil courts in the State. It has civil, criminal, probate and chancery jurisdiction. There are probably more individual cases filed in this Court than in any other court in the State, even where there are a number of judges presiding. It is in session steadily and constantly, from one end of the year to the other, with a short respite in the summer. At the present time, it is presided over by only one judge, who is also the judge of the Juvenile Court. There is hardly a day when the judge comes from the bench at 5 o'clock in the afternoon that his time is not engaged until 7 with some children's cases. His presence is necessitated at chambers at least four nights during the week. No such strenuous life could have been kept up were there not a joy, pleasure and enthusiasm in the children's work.

Under the law recently passed by the legislature an outside judge from another county can be called in, and the Court has been greatly assisted by Hon. Rice W. Means of Adams County, Hon. A. S. Frost of Teller County, Hon. Junius Anderson of Boulder, Hon. R. D. McLeod of Leadville and Hon. Charles E. Southard of Greeley.

Mr. O. S. Storrs, Mrs. Ida L. Gregory and Mr. Lilburn Merrill, the probation officers and attendants upon this Court, and Mr. E. L. Shaffer, deputy sheriff, are to be commended for their faithful and efficient service, as is also the much loved, faithful and honest old bailiff, Uncle John Murray, who, in his present position some twenty years ago, chased the present judge out of the court house when he, too, was one of the "kids," sliding down the same long banisters. He does not "fix" the boys now; he fixes the banisters.

The ladies of the West Side Neighborhood House have rendered us much help and assistance. That good woman, Mrs. Sarah Platt Decker, president of the National Federation of Woman's Clubs, and whom all Coloradoans love to honor, has ever been an active supporter of the Court, as has also Mrs. A. M. Dickinson, noted for her interest in reforms for the betterment of children.

The Court has nothing but the warmest commendation for all of its clerks and employes, who perform the clerical work of the civil divisions of the county court, and especially the chief clerk thereof, Thomas L. Bonfils, who, for devotion to the public service, efficiency and economy in office, has never been excelled in this State. It is largely through his untiring efforts that the judge of the Court has been able to give as much time as has been given to the cause of the children.

No more direct assistance has been received in the way of personal work than that of Mr. Charles H. Libby, the court reporter, who has ever been ready, day and night, to assist in the work of the Court.

It will thus be seen that the judge of the Juvenile Court of Denver is only a small factor in the far-reaching work that has been accomplished.

The following extract from a letter from Mr. Jacob Riis, the great reformer, to the writer, would seem, however, not to underestimate the importance of the judge, and may furnish the excuse for this report. He says: "I said it before and I repeat it, the whole life of this most far-reaching reform hangs upon the faithful execution of the probation law by the judges. They are the keepers of the people's conscience in this matter and have it in their power to smother or put it to sleep. Thank God for the judges who try to keep it awake."

President Roosevelt, whom we all know, said that Mr. Riis was "the most useful citizen of New York."

Mr. Riis ought to know what is useful, and he has said:

"The problem of the children is the problem of the State. As we mould the children of the toiling masses in our cities, so we shape the destiny of the State which they will rule in their turn, taking the reins from our hands. In proportion as we neglect or pass them by, the blame for bad government to come rests upon us."

And the last time President Roosevelt was in Colorado he said, speaking to our people:

"Just one word on the future of the country—the country as it will be twenty, thirty or forty years hence. A good deal depends upon how we handle business, how we do our great industrial work, how we handle the farms and ranches, but what counts most is the kind of men and women that there are at that time in the country. No nation is safe unless in the average family there are healthy and happy children. If these children are not brought up well, they are not merely a curse to themselves and their parents, but they mean the ruin of the State in the future."

And so it must become the belief of every earnest citizen interested in the home and the citizenship of tomorrow that questions of politics—the tariff, the money question, what is to be done with an alien race in the Philippines, or what not— cannot begin to compare in importance with the question of the children. A member of the President's cabinet recently said in a public address that the boys of America were the most neg- lected creatures in the world. I have seen them by the thousands and tens of thousands amidst the congested centers of popula- tion in all the great cities of the Union, and I know they do not receive near the attention given to live stock. The marvel is that they turn out as well as they do and that crime is no more prevalent than it is. The State is making magnificent efforts to provide for the intellectual welfare of its children, but it can never hope to get the best results from its labor unless this be supplemented by equal efforts for their moral welfare. The church and the school have a tremendous work, but when these and the home fail the State is called in, and after all the State is above the parent. It is its duty to see that the child is cared for. It can and does send the child to school or keep it from work, whether the parent consents or not. It does not ask the consent of the parent. The parent merely has the consent of the State to the custody of the child so long as it is to the child's best interest, and because of natural love and affection it is simply assumed that it is, till the contrary be shown. The State respects and encourages these natural ties, but parents have not owned their children since the days of Roman slavery, and when the parents shirk or fail and their influence degrades the child, their right to its care and custody may be forfeited to the State. Then the State must compel the parents to do their duty; in many cases it must assist; and, purely in the interest of the child, it must often properly and necessarily assume (not usurp) these functions. In doing this let it discharge its duty as nearly as possible as a wise and loving parent should—with patience, with justice, with charity, with love, and yet with firmness and with strength.

WHAT THE BOYS SAY.

At Christmas time I offered four prizes to the boys who would write the best letters upon the subject:

"What, in your opinion, causes boys to get into trouble—that is, 'swipe' things, play truant or do other bad things? Why do they do it? Are they more afraid of doing wrong or of getting caught? Is there, in your opinion, any difference between swiping an apple or a dollar? Will any of the boys you know 'swipe' things? Does it pay the judge to be square with a boy? Will most of them be square in return? What do you call being 'square' with the judge? Is it square to bring a poor report? Why do some boys bring poor reports?"

I did this because at each session of the Juvenile Court we have a Saturday morning talk in which such things are discussed and I was anxious to know what the boys thought about it.

We considered a number of things in awarding the prizes. One thing that struck us was the fact that of some fifty boys out of over one hundred, who are on probation and wrote letters, only one made any reference to God, the Bible or the Ten Commandments. This was the boy who won the prize. He wrote the letter while confined in the Detention School.

I am sure none of the boys had any assistance. The second best letter was written by a boy unusually bright for his age. It is written just as I have heard him talk—with a maturity beyond his years. I know quite a few other boys who have been in this court who could give some good advice to parents, and I hope they, as well as the boys, may read these letters.

We have withheld the names, not that there is anything to be ashamed of, but because we prefer to do so for other reasons. If I had my way about it, I would make a law forbidding the publication in any paper of the name of a boy ever arrested or accused of any kind of an offense.

FIRST PRIZE.

Denver, Colo., March 11, '04·

Mr. Judge Lindsey:

Dear Judge—In answer to yours of the 9th in regard to what causes a boy to get into trouble, the best explanation I can give is: Because he does not obey the Ten Commandments and he turns his mind away from God and towards Satan and obeys him—what he puts into his mind. Hoping that I may win the prize, I remain,

Yours respectfully,

E. J., age 11, Franklin School.

SECOND PRIZE.

Dear Judge—There are several reasons why boys get into trouble. The principal one is that a good many boys do not get the proper care, and don't have enough interest taken in them by their parents, and the average parent don't know that their boys know as much as they really do, and they don't keep after their children enough to see that their morals are kept perfect and upright.

A boy likes to be respected and in most cases he don't get the sympathy that he should get.

Another reason is the going with bad company and the desire to have some fun and excitement. If a poor boy swipes anything won't he sell it and have a good time with the money, which he don't often get? In reality there are very few really bad boys who realize what they are doing when they swipe something and who mean to be thieves. Most of the boys who get into trouble are merely mischievous and are just trying to have some fun. Some boys think that swiping an apple or a bag of peanuts is not wrong, but it is just as bad as swiping money. I go to a school which, by most people, is thought to be a law-abiding school, but two-thirds of the boys are mischievous and if they are mischievous won't they get into some kind of trouble? Of course there are some really bad boys who need to be sent to say that Judge Lindsey was not square so I think whatever he does is all right in most boys' opinion. I hope this is satisfactory. I remain yours,

S. H., age 11, Webster School.

CHAPTER IV

Facts and Figures

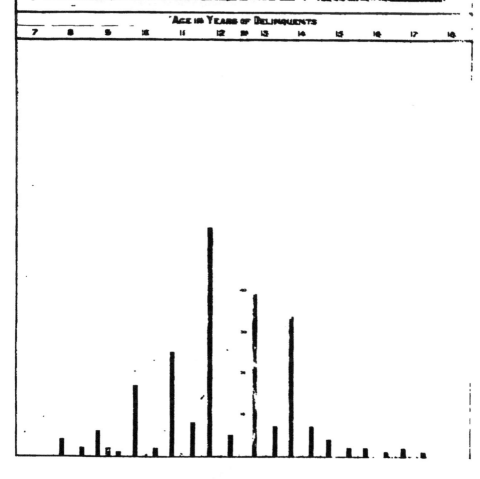

STATE OF COLORADO
CITY AND COUNTY OF DENVER
JUVENILE COURT

Chart showing the Number of Charges for Truancy during the
YEARS___ 1901 shown ▬▬▬▬▬ .1902 shown ═ ═ ═ .1903 shown ▬▬▬▬▬.

AGE IN YEARS OF DELINQUENTS

| 7 | 8 | 9 | 10 | 11 | 12 | 13 | 14 | 15 | 16 | 17 | 18 |

STATE OF COLORADO
CITY AND COUNTY OF DENVER
JUVENILE COURT

Chart showing Percentage of Commitments for Truancy during the
Years__ 1901.shown ▬▬▬ , 1902.shown ‾ _ ⁊;, 1903.shown ▬▬▬ .

AGE IN YEARS OF DELINQUENTS

7	8	9	10	11	12		13	14	15	16	17	18

FACTS AND FIGURES.
1903.

	Boys.	Girls.	Total.
Parents and children in Juvenile Court.. ...		...	495
Dependent children	37	23	60
Delinquent children	359	30	389
Parents of delinquent children; fathers, 23; mothers, 23.....................		...	46

DISPOSITION OF DEPENDENT CASES.

	Boys.	Girls.	Total.
Adopted into homes..................	15	15	30
Committed to State Home for Dependent Children	22	8	30

FORMS OF DELINQUENCY CHARGED.

Burglary	31
Larceny	113
Truancy	27
Disorderly conduct (including truancy).....................	40
Disorderly conduct..	178
Total......	389

AGES OF DELINQUENTS.

Years.	Boys.	Girls.	Total.
8	11		11
9	20	2	22
10	29	5	34
11	60	2	62
12	62	7	69
13	57	4	61
14	64	4	68
15	89	3	42
16	11	3	14
17	3		3
Total	359	30	389

DISPOSITION OF DELINQUENTS.

1903.	Boys.	Girls.	Total.
Tried by Court from January 1, 1903, to January 1, 1904..................	359	30	389
Delinquents charged with offenses not considered serious enough to require them to report....................	50	5	55
Dismissals	32	6	38
Committed to State Industrial School at the time of trial during same period.	8	3	11
Placed on probation during same period, without any commitment...........	231	16	247
Committed to State Industrial School for other offenses after being placed on probation (being 3.2 per cent.)......	9	...	9
Total number placed on probation.......	260	16	276
Total number committed to the Industrial School during the year........	17	3	20

CAUSES OF COMMITMENTS.

Forms of delinquencies, number and ages of boys committed to the State Industrial School from January 1, 1903, to January 1, 1904:

	Total.
Larceny—One 9 years of age, one 10 years of age, three 11 years of age, four 12 years of age, one 13 years of age, one 14 years of age, one 15 years of age...............	12
Disorderly Conduct—One 11 years of age, one 12 years of age	2
Truancy (including disorderly conduct)—Two 11 years of age	2

Girls committed during the same period:

Incorrigibility—One 10 years of age, two 16 years of age...	3

REPORT SYSTEM ADOPTED BY THIS COURT.

(Part of Probation System.)

1903.	Boys.	Girls.	Total.
Number of boys and girls now on the report list and required to report at the morning session of every Juvenile Court day (every other Saturday)	197	8	205
Number of reports from probationers received from school teachers during the year			2,275
Number of reports from other sources...			864
Total reports received............			3,139
Each report represents a personal interview between the Judge of the Court and probationer............			3,139
Baths given probationers during the year			1,150
Positions secured during the year.......			252
Boys sent to the beet fields for the summer			77
Needy children relieved...............			175
Number of garments supplied (second hand)			175
Number of garments supplied (new).....			220
Total garments supplied.............			395

RECORD OF PROBATIONS FOR 1901, 1902, AND 1903.

	Boys.	Girls.	Total.
Number placed on probation in 1901....	188	16	204
Number placed on probation in 1902....	327	23	350
Number placed on probation in 1903....	231	16	247
Total probationed	746	55	801

Probationers committed during the three years, all boys
(less than 5 per cent.)............................... 40

Most of the commitments made at the time of trial and not subjected to the probation sytem, were cases where the children in question had no home conditions, or where their environments were such as to make it unwise to submit them to the probation system.

VOLUNTARY DELINQUENTS AND PROBATIONERS.

There are over 200 boys who have come into the Juvenile Court within the last three years, termed "voluntary delinquents." These boys have been brought here principally by other boys who have been proceeded against in court. They often belong to some "gang," and have come in voluntarily and admitted various offenses against the law. They have not, as a rule, been tried, but have been assisted in various ways, and the great majority of them have reformed their habits entirely.

TOTAL NUMBER OF CHILDREN DEALT WITH IN THE JUVENILE COURT DURING THE YEARS 1901, 1902, 1903.

	Boys.	Girls.	Total.
Total number of dependent children...	98	83	181
Delinquent children	1,014	90	1,104
			1,285

Voluntary delinquent boys.............................. 200

Total number of children in the Juvenile Court in three
years 1,485

LITERATURE DISTRIBUTED EACH MONTH.

Copies.

Current number of "Success"............................ 100
Current number of "American Boy".................... 100
Current number of "Men of Tomorrow"................. 100

———

Total monthly copies............................... 300

To which is occasionally added "The Youth's Companion" and other healthful publications.

It is gratifying to report that the boys in court are doing as much as any other power to enforce obedience to the law among juveniles, on the theory that the court is for their benefit and assistance, and loyalty to it demands in return their assistance; first, in keeping out of mischief themselves; and, second, in discouraging law-breaking among their companions.

STATE OF COLORADO
CITY AND COUNTY OF DENVER
JUVENILE COURT

Chart showing the Number of Charges for Larceny during the
YEARS – 1901, shown ▬▬▬ ;1902, shown   ,1903, shown ▬▬▬ .

AGE IN YEARS OF DELINQUENTS.

7	8	9	10	11	12	13	14	15	16	17	18

STATE OF COLORADO
CITY AND COUNTY OF DENVER
JUVENILE COURT

Chart showing Percentage of Commitments for Larceny during the
YEARS___1901.shown ▄▄▄▄▄ ,1902.shown ∙∙∙∙∙∙ ,1903.shown ▄▄▄▄▄ .

AGE IN YEARS OF DELINQUENTS

7	8	9	10	11	12	%	13	14	15	16	17	18

A LESSON FROM THE FIGURES.

As showing the "mischievous age" or dangerous age in child life the following chart showing the ages of 1,000 delinquents covering a period of three years is instructive. It will be seen that the greatest numbers are at 12 and 14:

AGES OF DELINQUENTS--1901, 1902, 1903.

Age.	Boys.	Girls.	Total.
8	19		19
9	31	3	34
10	79	6	85
11	120	3	123
12	147	13	160
13	163	21	184
14	178	11	189
15	134	8	142
16	33	11	44
17	12	8	20
	916	84	1,000

MONTHLY REPORTS BY PROBATION OFFICERS.

In order that some idea may be had of the routine work in the Juvenile Court a few monthly reports are herewith submitted. Indicating as they do, a great deal of work, they only convey an inadequate idea of the enormous amount of work done. Heretofore such work in a city has been largely neglected or not done at all until criminals are made, when we spend thousands to convict them. A report marked "poor" by a teacher only indicates a breach of some little rule of discipline in school and not a repeated offense. Three-fourths of the "poor" reports are for "whispering" or similar offense. As most boys who get into court are usually lively and mischievous it makes the showing all the more creditable. Boys report at the meetings of probationers with the judge every two weeks.

PROBATION OFFICER'S REPORT FOR FEBRUARY, 1904.

Reports from teachers................written, 300; verbal, 23

	Feb. 13.	Feb. 27.
Good	121	119
Excellent	11	12
Fair	13	22
Poor	9	16
	154	169

Total 323

Number of boys excused from reporting.................. 6

Number of girls excused................................ 1

Number of boys committed to State Industrial School...... 3

Number of boys committed after having been placed on probation 2

Number of boys committed at time of trial............... 1

Number of boys tried in court............................ 61

Number of cases settled out of court.................... 82

Complaints heard in office............................. 86

Letters written to boys............................... 283

Letters written to parents............................. 150

Letters written—applications for positions.............. 18

Situations obtained 10

Number of physical examinations........................ 4

Visits made to homes................................. 96

Visits made to schools................................ 12

Visits made to dance halls............................. 3

Visits made to slums................................. 12

Saloons investigated 5

Number of boys brought into court...................... 77

    Number placed on probation...................... 13

    Number fined and the sentence suspended............ 2

    Number brought into court by city railroad company for hopping cars, organized into Little Citizens' League for Law Enforcement and discharged..... 62

Number of parents brought into court for contributing to the delinquency of children........................ 11

Mothers 3
    Discharged 0
    Fined 2
    Suspended 1
Fathers 8
    Discharged 0
    Suspended 0
    Fined 8
Other than parents................................... 0
Total number contributing to the delinquency of children.. 11
Number of working boys on probation list............... 51
Number of school boys on probation list................. 153
Shoes furnished to children (pairs)...................... 10
Suits furnished to children............................. 7
Needy cases relieved................................... 40
Baths given 100

PROBATION OFFICER'S REPORT FOR MARCH, 1904.

Reports from teachers.................................. 281
Verbal reports 23

                           ———

    Total 304

	Mar. 12.	Mar. 26.
Good	112	94
Excellent	12	5
Fair	28	21
Poor	16	16
	168	136

    Total 304
Number of boys excused from reporting................. 19
Number of boys on trial............................... 33
Number of boys committed to State Industrial School...... 4
Number of parents contributing to the delinqnecy of children 10
    Fathers 6
        Fined and suspended.............................. 3
        Discharged 2
        Fired 1

Mothers 4

    Discharged 2

    Fined and suspended............................. 2

Number other than parents........................ 2

    Sentenced to jail............................... 2

Total number contributing to delinquency of children...... 12

Number of letters to boys............................. 30

Number of letters to parents........................ 8

Number of letters—applications for positions............ 28

Complaints heard in office............................ 83

Situations obtained 23

Adoption cases recorded.............................. 6

Dependent cases recorded............................ 4

Number of children brought into court.................. 37

Number of children ordered to report................... 13

Number discharged 2

Number of cases fined and fine remitted................. 22

Number of working boys on list....................... 44

Number of school boys on list......................... 153

Number of garments furnished needy families............ 127

Shoes furnished to boys (pairs)........................ 8

Suits furnished to boys............................... 3

Needy cases relieved................................. 21

Baths given, about................................... 100

PROBATION OFFICER'S REPORT FOR APRIL, 1904.

Reports from teachers................................. 187

Verbal reports 21

Total 208

	April 9.	April 23.
Good	76	59
Excellent	5	8
Fair	14	33
Poor	1	12
	96	112
Total		208

Number of boys on trial.................................   24
Number of boys excused   10
Number of girls committed to State Industrial School.....   1
Number of parents contributing to the delinquency of chil-
    dren   3
        Fathers (fined)   2
        Mothers (discharged)   1
Number of letters to boys..............................   17
Number of letters to parents...........................   8
Complaints heard in office.............................   73
Letters written—applications for positions..............   16
Situations obtained   12
Adoption cases recorded...............................   1
Dependent cases recorded.............................   3
Number of children brought into court..................   26
Number of children fined..............................   1
Number of children placed on probation and ordered to
    report   11
Number discharged   14
Number of working boys on probation list...............   48
Number of school boys on probation list................   179
Number of garments furnished to needy families.........   89
Shoes furnished to boys (pairs).........................   6
Suits furnished to boys................................   2
Cases settled out of court.............................   63
Number of cases released and sent home.................   9
Number of physical examinations.......................   1
Average number of boys held at Detention School........   37
Number of girls held at Detention School...............   0
Baths given   100

PROBATION OFFICER'S REPORT, MAY, 1904.
OFFICE.

Reports from teachers..................................   226
Verbal   50
                                                            —
                                                            276

	May 7.	May 21.
Good	77	65
Excellent	11	10
Fair	45	41
Poor	14	13
	147	129

Total	276
Number of children excused May 7	13
Number of boys excused May 21	7
Total number excused	20
Number of boys on trial	41
Number of girls on trial	2
Total	43
Number of children placed on probation and ordered to report	27
Discharged	4
Sent to Detention School and suspended	5
Sent to Detention School	1
Cases continued	6
Physical examinations by Dr. Hopkins	6
Number of parents brought into court for contributing to delinquency of children	4
Mothers	1
Fathers	3
Discharged	1
Fined	1
Jail sentence	1
Jail sentence (served)	1
Number of letter written to boys	295
Number of letters written to parents	10
Complaints heard in office	89
Cases settled out of court	42
Letters written—applications for positions	10
Situations obtained	4
Number of school boys on probation list	153
Number of working boys on probation list	44
Number of dependent cases recorded	2

Shoes furnished to boys (pairs)......................... 4

Suits furnished to boys................................. 1

Needy families relieved................................ 10

Children committed to Woodcroft Home for Feeble Minded. 4

Runaways returned to homes outside of State........... 2

Baths given 120

CHAPTER V

The Expense

THE EXPENSE.

In considering the question of expense it would be well first to make a conservative estimate of the cost to the State to detect, convict and care for criminals. We have, therefore, consulted the city, county and State records and conferred with the wardens of state prisons, the district attorney's office, sheriffs and police departments and obtained the estimates herein as rather under than over the real expenses. It should be borne in mind that children under the juvenile law can no longer be cared for in jails or the criminal courts, so that the figures here given for jails and criminal courts represent the cost for those other than children coming under the juvenile class.

MONEY INVESTED IN JAILS IN DENVER.

County jail, buildings and grounds...................$200,000
City jail, buildings and grounds..................... 50,000

Total $250,000

ANNUAL EXPENDITURE FOR MAINTENANCE OF JAILS AND CRIMINAL COURTS IN DENVER.

County jail—salaries of jailers, board of prisoners,
    maintenance, etc. ....$ 40,000
City jail—salaries and expenditures................. 15,000
Policemen and detectives' salaries................. 155,000
District attorney's office to prosecute................ 20,000
Criminal court—judges, clerks, juries, witnesses and
    officials 50,000

Total $280,000
Amount permanently invested in Denver to care for
    criminals 250,000
Interest on total sum at 5 per cent................... 26,500

Total annual expense and investment in Denver for
    care of criminals............................$556,500

We have not at hand as accurate figures of the cost of crime in the State outside of Denver, yet it may be reasonably estimated as follows:

Investment in buildings, grounds and equipments, penitentiary and reformatory combined...............$650,000

Annual cost of both institutions, at least............. 150,000

Expense annually for crime outside of Denver in State for courts, officers, keep of prisoners in jails, etc., estimated to be at least........................ 300,000

Invested in jails in State outside of Denver, estimated at least 350,000

Total invested in prisons and jails in State outside of Denver $1,000,000

Total annual expense of crime in State outside of Denver 450,000

Of course this does not include cost to victims and many other sources of expense almost impossible to compute.

Figures outside of Denver in the State are not all accessible, but anyone familiar with the prison condition, criminal courts and police departments of this State, must know that the real facts would show an amount considerably in excess of that here estimated. The police department annual appropriation for the year 1904 in Denver is actually $200,000, though here estimated at much less, and in 1903 alone, the legislature appropriated $200,000 for the penitentiary, largely for buildings, repairs, etc.

In considering the expense of the Juvenile Court of Denver a few things are important to bear in mind:

First—For nearly three years the Juvenile Court was conducted without any paid probation officers or the expense of a Detention School.

Second—Instead of creating a new court with its special judge, clerk and court officials, as has been done in Indianapolis, Indiana (about the size of Denver), Baltimore, Maryland, and some other cities, with the added expense of salaries for the judge and other officials, we have put the entire work in a court already created without any additional expense of judge, clerks, bailiffs, etc. This work has simply been added to that of these officials without any extra compensation. It is not claimed that this is just, or that it should not be remedied, since the criminal courts have thus been relieved of probably one-fourth of their work, but it is stated as the fact for the time this report covers.

Third—Under the fee system the county paid fees for juvenile cases, but the amount returned by the court earned from other litigants more than offsets this expense So that the expense for the first three years of the Juvenile Court was practically nothing, certainly not to exceed two or three hundred dollars, notwithstanding the Governor, in his message to the Assembly at the end of the first eighteen months of the court, declared it had saved over $88,000 to the people by reduced expense in incarcerations and commitments to institutions, with a showing of ten times as many successful corrections among juvenile offenders.

At present under the new laws the added annual expense incurred by the Juvenile Court is as follows:

Three paid probation officers $3,900
Maintenance of Detention School, as estimated for salaries of employes and keep of inmates............. 5,000
Incidental expenses 1,000

Total $9,900
To the above expense a clerk of the Juvenile Court will be appointed, beginning June 1st, 1904, at an annual salary of $1,500

The salary of the judge is not included, as this expense always existed in the court proper, and is more than earned in the civil business of the court. In the criminal court one judge is constantly engaged in criminal cases. This is not true of the Juvenile Court.

Assuming, however, that the cost of the Juvenile Court of Denver was twice, even five times as much, as now estimated, would it not be more than justifiable? Our opinion is that an expenditure of $20,000 per annum at the present time, to bring the Juvenile Court system nearer perfection, would be the best investment the city and county could make. For every thousand dollars thus spent there will be in course of time at least ten thousand dollars saved.

Two immense savings in dollars and cents have been made in the Juvenile Court during the last three years:

First—In correcting children offenders in the home without the necessity of sending so many to jails and institutions at the expense of the State, as formerly, thus greatly reducing commitments in proportion to children brought into court.

Second—Dispensing with the expense of erecting and maintaining a parental or truant school, provided for by the Legislature three years ago.

The following is taken from the report of the Juvenile Court for 1902:

COMPARISON OF EXPENSE AND RESULTS OBTAINED UNDER OLD SYSTEM AND THE PRESENT.

"The results obtained under the present system of dealing with juveniles, as compared with former methods employed, are so extremely gratifying as to justify serious consideration. Under the probation system established by this Court during the past eighteen months, including the report system, the commitments to the Industrial School from this Court have decreased over 50 per cent., as compared with the prior eighteen months, while operating under the same law. The results as compared with the old methods of the criminal courts of this county are even more gratifying.

"The enormous expense to State and county for the prosecution and punishment of criminals is seldom considered and little realized by the ordinary citizen. Any system which tends to reduce such expense is a benefit to the State. Yet infinitely more far-reaching than the actual expense saved is the moral effect, which tends to make a higher and better citizenship. The results of the work of juvenile courts in this respect are little appreciated because not generally understood. Prior to the enactment of the compulsory education law in 1899, children complained against for those offenses termed criminal by the law, were tried in the criminal division of the District Court, with the attendant associations with adult hardened criminals, its baneful effects of jail life, which tends more in most cases to make the child a criminal than the offense for the commission of which it was charged. The result was, prosecutions were only had in the exceptional and severe cases, the grand jury often refusing to indict, or the prosecuting officer to inform against, because of the tender age of the offender, it being a choice of evils between the system of prosecution then in vogue and permitting the child to go without the correcting restraint contemplated by the law. No definite record has been kept in this county of the number of such cases, but there seems to be sufficient definite information in other jurisdictions from which interesting and safe deductions may be drawn. From a report relating to the operation of juvenile courts, published in a recent issue of the 'Juvenile Court Record' of Chicago, Illinois, it is stated that prior to the enactment of the juvenile court law in Illinois, there were hundreds of boys under sixteen years of age in Chicago indicted by the grand jury each year for burglary, petit depredations upon railroad property, candy and bake shops, and other offenses which, in most cases, might justly be considered the result of boyish pranks or exuberance leading to thoughtlessness rather than crime. Many such unfortunate youths remained in jail for months awaiting the action of the grand jury, and yet 75 per cent. of the cases were thrown out because of the tender age of the alleged offenders. This condition of affairs was first strikingly brought to the attention of the authorities in Chicago by that splendid woman, the mother of the juvenile court of Illinois, Mrs. Lucy L. Flower. 'The deplorable fact must be admitted, however,' continues the report, 'that most of the 75 per cent. turned loose by the grand jury eventually were returned and indicted later for repeated offenses.' It appears clearly, therefore, that this serious defect can only be corrected by the enactment of laws establishing a juvenile court and probation system. It was also repeatedly stated in the same publication that 17,000 boys were dealt with by the criminal courts and jails in one year in Chicago before the juvenile law.

"The Clerk of the Criminal Division of the District Court of Denver, for the purpose of a fair comparison as here pointed out, selected from the records of former years of that Court fifteen cases of individual boys under sixteen years of age charged and convicted of burglary and larceny. The detailed statement furnished by him shows that for convicting these fifteen boys the County of Arapahoe paid in court and jury fees alone the sum of $638.05, an average in each case of $42.53. These figures do not include the jailer's fees, the cost of incarceration in State institutions or mileage fees paid for transportation. Yet, twelve of these fifteen boys thus convicted in the Criminal Court were committed to such institutions. The cost of transportation to the Reformatory at Buena Vista for each prisoner is $72.85, according to figures furnished us. The per capita expense at Buena Vista was $418; at the Industrial School at Golden, $200 per year. The average time of incarceration at such institutions is at least one year in each case. This does not take into consideration what is in the long run of infinitely more importance, namely, the evils to the child itself.

"THE CASE OF ONE BOY.

"To illustrate, take the case of John C., one of the fifteen boys here referred to. He is now sixteen years of age. In 1898, at the age of twelve years, he was tried and convicted in this county and sentenced to jail, for a petit theft from a grocery store. The boy is a naturally bright, well-meaning Scandinavian lad. In our opinion more as a result of his first experience in jail than any natural viciousness, he has been arrested for burglary and larceny down to the present time as follows: Twice in 1899; five times in 1900; once in 1901 and once in 1902. He has been in jail nine times and in the Industrial School twice during that period. It is safely estimated from the records that correcting this boy by such methods cost the State and county $782 at least. Last February this boy was serving a sentence in jail for burglary, after trial and conviction in the Criminal Division of the District Court. His release was obtained by the officers of the Juvenile Court. A good position was secured for him, and though he has had the 'moving about fever' twice, he has been returned without expense to the county or State, and is now a faithful, working boy, with every prospect of reform. Of course, some care and patience is required in such a case. But is not such care and patience justifiable, as well as the wisest economy to the State? It is rather the exception that we encounter serious difficulties with cases of this character, but we are bound to have disappointments in many cases and complete failure in some. But such failures do not begin to compare with the failures under the old system, and in no case could failure be near so serious in its effects and results. It seems strange and inconsistent that while the State provides by law ample funds for the maintenance of the old system, and liberal pay for the officials acting under it, it provides not one cent for the probation system here referred to.

"COMPARATIVE TABLES OF EXPENSE.

"To summarize the cost of convicting and punishing these fifteen boys, we may safely calculate as follows:

Actual court costs	$ 638.05
Cost of transportation	60.00
Eleven sent to Industrial School for average period of one year each	2,200.00
One sent to Buena Vista, transportation and mileage fees	72.85
Expense of incarceration	418.00
Two committed to County Jail for an average of 60 days each	30.00
	$3,418.90

"Sentence was suspended in one case of the fifteen to which we referred.

"It will thus be seen that it cost the people an average of $227.92 for each boy thus dealt with in the Criminal Court under the old system.

"To compare with this statement of expense, as a fair average, we have also selected at random the cases of fifteen boys in the Juvenile Court, convicted of identically the same offenses, regarded, however, as disorderly conduct. The total aggregate court costs, including fees of every character paid by the county, is the sum of $179.85, or an average of $11.89 for each boy. Taking the 560 cases of delinquent children referred to in this report and subtracting therefrom truancy and other cases, we have 454 boys tried in the Juvenile, which, under the old system, could only have been tried in the Criminal Court, unless, as was frequently the case, no prosecution was instituted because of the tender age of the offender. But, as already shown by the Chicago report referred to, most of such cases would eventually, at a later age, because of such neglect, return to be prosecuted in the Criminal Courts. We may, therefore, fairly summarize the following comparative cost to the people for dealing alone with the cases prosecuted during the past eighteen months:

454 boys tried and disposed of in the Juvenile Division of the County Court during the last eighteen months. If tried under the old system in the Criminal Court on the basis of actual average costs of fifteen cases actually tried there, would incur an expense to the county and State of an average of $227.92 per capita, or a total for 454 cases $103,475.68

Same cases tried in the Juvenile Court under the probation system and disposed of at the following fairly estimated expense to State and county (incarcerations for average of one year, figured in both cases). Total court costs of 454 cases $5,448.00
Incarcerations, 46 in number........... 9,200.00

Total cost to county and State.....$14,648.00   14,648.00

Total saving to county and State in eighteen months by prosecuting said cases in Juvenile Division of County Court $88,827.68

"The entire court costs, district attorney's fees, etc., incurred by the county for juvenile cases in the Juvenile Division of this Court are more than paid by the surplus earnings of the other divisions of the Court, to be eventually returned to the County. So that the juvenile cases here reported have not cost the county one cent. The expense of incarcerations is a State expense."

STATE OF COLORADO
CITY AND COUNTY OF DENVER
JUVENILE COURT

Expense Chart.

Under Criminal Court	Under Juvenile Court
15 Cases, Chosen at random, cost State and County ___ $1,415.00.	15 Cases, Chosen at random, cost State and County ___ $175.85.
Cost per Capita, ___ $ 397.00	Cost per Capita, ___ $ 11.80.
All committed to Institutions.	All placed on Probation.

—— Saving in favor of Juvenile Court.
—— $3,250.85. ——

Number of Delinquent Boys tried in Juvenile Court during last 18 Months. ___ 454.

Under Criminal Court these 454 Cases, at the above per capita, would have cost the State and County ___ $105,475.00.	Actual Cost of these 454 cases under Juvenile Court, including 46 commitments to Industrial School. ___ $14,848.00.

Saving in favor of Juvenile Court. —
—— $88,827.00. ——

—— — Note. —— — —

Juvenile Court expense is covered by the surplus earnings of the other divisions of the Court.

Incarceration is a State Expense.

Estimated on the above figures we might calculate as follows, for three years, including only cases where the delinquency charged otherwise was a crime (not including truancy):

849 boys tried and disposed of in the Juvenile Division of the County Court during the past three years. If tried under the old system in the Criminal Court on the basis of actual average costs of fifteen similar cases of boys actually tried there for crime, would incur an expense to the county and State of an average of $227.92 per capita, or a total sum of........................$193,504.04

Same cases tried in the Juvenile Court, under the probation system and disposed of at the following fairly estimated expense to State and county (incarcerations of average of one year figured in both cases). Total court costs of 849 cases, $11.89 per capita.. $10,094.61

Incarcerations, 105 in number, including all incarcerations out of the entire 1,369 boys at the Juvenile Court in three years (State expense).........21,000.00
                                                    ————————
Total cost to county and State, 3 years. 31,094.61. $31,094.61
                                                    ————————

Total saving to county and State in three years by prosecuting said cases in Juvenile Division of County Court...............$162,509.47

As pointed out, the $10,094.61 paid to the Court in three years as fees or costs for the juvenile cases has been more than earned by the court from civil litigants under the fee system of the courts of Colorado above all expenses, and actually has been paid to the county, so that it may be properly eliminated, making the total saving in this item alone (which does not include the $125,000 hereafter shown saved by doing away with the parental school) of $172,509.47

There is no possible escape from crediting the Juvenile Court and the probation and report system for the saving of the second item of expense, namely, the parental school. In 1901, before the present report and probation system in the Juvenile Court was perfected, it was shown to the Legislature that there were one or two hundred habitual truants each year in Denver, and to care for them a parental school was necessary. The bill was passed, making it mandatory to establish the school at once. As a result of the Juvenile Court work described in this report, it has been unnecessary. Allowing for the maintenance of such a school, salaries of teachers and keep of children, an annual expense of $25,000 per annum, and in case a special school was built, at least $50,000, would have been necessary therefor. In three years this saving has therefore approximated $125,000. And just so long as the building and maintenance of this institution can be reasonably deferred under the present system, just so long do we continue to save a similar annual expense, more than double in any one year all that the Juvenile Court system now costs.

SUMMARY.

The following summary should be an object lesson to those who object to spending money for the proper correction and saving of children:

INVESTMENTS IN DENVER.

County jail, buildings and grounds	$200,000
City jail, buildings and grounds	50,000
Total	$250,000

DETENTION HOUSE.

Rental per annum	$ 900
Furniture and fixtures	1,000
Total	$ 1,900

ANNUAL EXPENSE

To detect, convict and care for criminals in Denver.	$280,000
To care for children offenders	9,900

8

SAVING IN EXPENSE TO TAXPAYERS OF CITY, COUNTY AND STATE FOR THREE YEARS BY JUVENILE COURT.

Saving from parental school $125,000.00

Saving in reduced commitments and expense of court proceedings; all children's cases taken from criminal and police courts $172,509.47

TOTAL SAVING by Juvenile Court system in three years $297,509.47

Less expense of maintenance during same time, which expense has only existed for past year, at $9,900 .... 9,900.00

$287,609.47

TOTAL COST to taxpayers in Denver to detect, convict and care for criminals through the criminal courts for same three years (not including State expense at either the penitentiary or reformatory —some $200,000 more) $840,000.00

It is important to recall in this connection that one-half of all the inmates of all prisons (jails and penitentiaries combined) are said by eminent authorities to be under twenty-three years of age, which shows that within a very few years before they were mere boys needing earnest, painstaking, scientific care and handling under such a system as the Juvenile Court provides, and not the brutal bungling of the jail and the criminal courts. Again, as already pointed out, in nearly all cities from one-fifth to one-fourth of all the arrests (excluding drunks) are among minors, mere boys of the city.

SOME DEDUCTIONS.

Three years' history in the Juvenile Court and crime in Denver (it has really been nearer four years) in considering the question of expense on the basis of the figures furnished, afford some interesting deductions.

In the first place, any experienced police official will tell you that over one-half of their troubles come from "these young fellows—little more than kids," as they have so often expressed it to me from New York to San Francisco in every large city in whose jails I have been and talked with the officers. This was the expression to me of an officer at the Tombs in New York, of jailer John L. Whitman in Chicago, of Sergeant James Dawson of St. Louis, Chief of Police Hayes of Kansas City, Chiefs of Police Michael Delaney and Hamilton Armstrong of Denver and Sergeant Bainbridge of San Francisco. All of these men are old and experienced officials. Dawson has had twenty-five years and Bainbridge thirty-five years' police experience. They will all tell you it is generally the "young fellows." I believe the Pinkertons will tell you the same thing in a way. Surely the young fellows were only boys yesterday.

How then should the expense be apportioned as between saving and condemning? Take the period of three years in Denver and we have:

ACTUALLY PAID to detect and convict crime in
Denver alone $840,000.00

ESTIMATED EXPENSE to care for and keep the
criminals sent to the penitentiary from Denver
during three years for varying periods from one
year to life imprisonment. There are about 700
inmates in the pen during this period, and Denver with nearly one-third of the population of
the State can be counted on to send this proportion of the prisoners at about $150.00 per capita
for keep for an average period of five years each. 175,000.00

INMATES of State Reformatory (branch of penitentiary) 145, and Denver furnishing about one-
third at cost of $277.00 per capita for average
period of 18 months 20,000.00
_____

Total $1,035,000.00

It is therefore easy to fairly estimate that with the State expense added it has cost the people at least one million dollars cash for crime during the three years last past in Denver alone.

Of course similar cost, probably greater, can be shown in other cities, for whatever is said of Denver pertains equally to them.

And if we have generally in cities one-fifth of all arrests among the youth under twenty and even under seventeen years of age (as I have found in some cities), would it be asking too much for one-fifth of the expenditure to save children? And if conceded, during the past three years, instead of spending less than $10,000 to save children in Denver, in dealing with crime, had the same proportion of expense been maintained we should have spent one-fifth of $840,000 or $168,000, and we do not here take into account the extra expense to the State this $840,000 necessitated. And yet from the small investment of less than $10,000 in three years to correct and care for children rightly, we show a saving of nearly $300,000 in three years. But call it $150,000 (impossible to get away from), or even nothing, could we have made a better investment?

None of these estimates take into any account the two most important savings in the problem, namely:

1st. The saving of the individual to good citizenship and society and all those unknown thousands whom the influence of a bad life unchecked would have led into crime.

2nd. The saving in dollars and cents in all the future years by the reduction of criminals and prevention of crime.

EXPENSIVE BOYS.

I recall a boy just past fifteen when first brought to the Juvenile Court with his pal three years ago, who had cost the County and State $1,036, which we figured up from the records of the police and criminal courts where he was often prosecuted. The expense for his pal was a close second. To-day one of these boys is getting $2.00 per day on one of our railroads and has cost the State nothing. Since he came to us the other thousand dollar specimen has not worked so well, but at least has never been re-arrested or cost the State one cent. But it has taken personal work, time and patience. Had these two boys originally, in their tender years of ten and eleven, been brought to a Juvenile Court and its earnest work, instead of the criminal court and indifferent jail methods, sufficient money alone would have been saved to have employed two probation officers for nearly a year.

People who call the Juvenile Court a fad are those who either do not know, do not understand, or do not care.

CHAPTER VI

The Court Approved

THE COURT APPROVED.

POLITICAL APPROVAL OF COURT.

Judge Lindsey was renominated in May, 1904, for Judge of the County and Juvenile Court by every political convention (seven in all) excepting the Socialists, who approved the Court, but could only put Socialists on their party ticket. At the election he received all the 56,000 votes cast, excepting less than one thousand cast for the Socialist candidate, thus attesting the popular approval of the Juvenile Court.

ENDORSEMENT OF POLICE DEPARTMENT.
OFFICE OF CHIEF OF POLICE.

Hon. Ben B. Lindsey, Judge County Court, City:

My Dear Judge—I desire to express to you my appreciation of your work with the boys of this city. As a member of the police department for several years, I have had an opportunity of watching your work in this line and observing the results. I also desire to compliment you, and I assure you that you shall have my sincere and hearty support in your work as long as I may hold the position of chief of police, for I realize what a task you have in this matter, and as your sincere friend I am only too anxious to do everything that either I or any of my men can do to further the wonderful results which you have thus far attained. The Juvenile Court is an unqualified success. We appreciate more and more every year that you are getting at this thing right and in the end will do more to reduce crime than all the criminal courts we have.

Wishing you continued success, I am

Sincerely yours,

M. A. DELANEY,

Chief of Police.

Denver, Colo.

OFFICE OF CITY CLERK.

Hon. Ben B. Lindsey,

Judge of the County Court,

City and County of Denver.

Dear Sir:

I have been watching with great interest the good you have been doing in that branch of your court known as

"The Juvenile Court," and take this opportunity to express to you my commendation of your great effort in behalf of the young wayward people of our city and county, and I assure you that I can speak from experience of the great benefit derived during my time as clerk of the police department of the City and County of Denver. It was my experience that we had more trouble and annoyance from the young people between the ages of eight and sixteen than all the other criminals put together, who were brought to my attention.

As I have not been connected with the police department for some time past, and during which time you have been pursuing your good work, I have taken the opportunity to examine the police records and I find that the annoyance from that source has almost ceased, and I am sure it is due to your great effort along this line, and that it is appreciated by the police department. It certainly must be very gratifying to the parents of the young boys of Denver to know that you have so earnestly enlisted your service in their behalf, which has resulted in taking many a young boy from a vicious life and starting him on his journey in the right direction. I sincerely trust that there may be nothing to deter you from the right step you have taken and trust you may continue the good work so nobly started.

I wish to say in conclusion that you will always find me ever ready to lend you any assistance in my power to further this good work.

Yours very respectfully,

E. E. SOMMERS,
Clerk, City and County of Denver.

MATRON, POLICE DEPARTMENT.

Chief's Office.

Hon. Ben B. Lindsey,
City.

Dear Sir:—I consider the Juvenile Court a great benefit to the wayward boys and girls of Denver. The report system has been unusually satisfactory and successful.

I have been Matron at the City Hall for almost six years. I had charge of the boys under sixteen years of age, so I am acquainted with the most of those who are on probation and take a great interest in them.

We do not have half as many boys placed under our care by the police as we did two years ago, and I attribute the fact to the manner in which the Juvenile Court is conducted.

IMOGENE G. CLARKE,
Police Matron.

UNION PACIFIC SYSTEM.

Office of Assistant Special Agent.

Hon. Ben. B. Lindsey,
    Judge Juvenile Court.

My Dear Judge:—As Chief Officer of the Special Secret Service of the Union Pacific Railroad Company, for this division, I desire to express to you my appreciation for and commendation of the Juvenile Court and its services and efforts on behalf of the juveniles of this city and county.

The railroad companies have for years been subject to depredations of boys, who have committed all sorts of depredations against the property of the company, from breaking into cars and robbing them of their contents and the stealing of the brass attachments off the cars. I desire to state to you that since the adoption by you of the methods of placing these boys, whom we have arrested and have tried before you, on probation and compelling them to attend school and report to you each two weeks, that our trouble with this class of offenders has been largely and almost 'entirely done away with. *In fact, our losses from this class of thieves have been reduced at least ninety per cent.*, and the boys who' formerly were ringleaders and really caused these depredations are now seldom seen around our tracks or property of the company, and on each of the reporting days in your Court I can point out the boys who have caused all this trouble.

The officers of the company approve the work of the Juvenile Court in this direction and wish to express to you their thanks for it. It is having a most beneficial influence on this class of boys, and if continued would prove of inestimable value and make good citizens of boys who, otherwise, would undoubtedly have grown up in a career of crime and ended in the State penitentiary.

Again thanking you, I beg to remain,

Very respectfully,

J. W. PENROSE,

Chief Officer.

Office Department Stores Detective.

Hon. Ben B. Lindsey, County Judge, Denver, Colorado:

My Dear Judge—It gives me unqualified satisfaction to inform you that none of your wards have left their reservation for a long time, and that the part of the city known as department stores, which until last year were their supposed privileged grounds, have not even seen a hunting party. We can now turn out our toy play sheep, tin soldiers and woolly dogs, bears, wild cats, deer, etc., without fear of loss or molestation. We even dare to leave children's marbles, spring guns, locomotives, trains of cars and candy, carelessly about, and none, so far, have been missing. This line of stock, as you may imagine, always has had a peculiar fascination for some of our youngsters, and I cannot quite understand the influence you must have brought to bear on them that such magnificent results have been attained.

I can assure you that it has saved our scouts a great deal of hard work in rounding up these culprits. You, of course, understand that this species of petty larceny has been with us an exceedingly mixed question to deal with. What to do with the boys after we have caught them was the burning question. We believe that you have solved it absolutely and the proper way to deal with them; yet I confess that I feel like taking my hat off to you and saying that your persistent efforts have awakened in the minds of these children not only a keen discrimination between right and wrong, but as well in that of all thinking people, the necessity of a broad charity—that they were once young themselves and likewise erred.

I desire to compliment you earnestly for this grand work you have begun, and to prophesy that this movement so aus-

¡ ciously commenced will stimulate a movement universal toward the fair, humane and wise treatment of juveniles that will ripen into perfection, or as near perfection as can be had.

Sincerely yours,

H. E. BURLEW,

Denver Department Stores Detective.

THE COLORADO & SOUTHERN RAILWAY COMPANY.

Office of General Superintendent.

Hon. Ben B. Lindsey,

County Judge, Denver.

Dear Sir:—Believing that the efforts of the Juvenile Court at reformation among the youths of this city should receive recognition, we desire, on behalf of the Special Service Department of The Colorado & Southern Railway Company, to express our sincere approval of your method of handling juvenile offenders.

For a long time boys kept organizing in gangs in various parts of the city, and they vied with each other in daringness on their thieving expeditions throughout the railway yards, and we know the railroads alone did not suffer, as the lads were frequently caught breaking into residences, their work often puzzling the authorities as to whether or not the acts were committed by adults, professionals in their business, as many boys had become adepts in pilfering houses, and their shrewdness in covering up their tracks would have done credit to much older heads.

Hardly a day passes but we encounter a once hopeless "hard case." We meet them on the streets selling papers; also, employed in shops, stores, etc., and they do not attempt to avoid meeting us, but approach us smilingly, as a repentant child confronts a forgiving parent.

The citizens of Denver ought to be thankful for the change wrought in so short a time in staying the alarming increase of so many bright boys starting in an evil course. We know of our own knowledge of some several hundred boys who have listened to your honor's fatherly advice, and they have not yet ten the promises you exacted of them before leaving the room—their present conduct being beyond criticism. For elfare of the children and our desire to co-operate with honor in this humane work, we endeavor, in many in- es, not to burden the Court with small cases, and often t the urchin home for their parents to chastise. This saves ι labor and expense to the county, and it is seldom that the . so treated repeats the offense.

Hoping the good work will go on uninterrupted, we as- you our hearty support and to assist in reforming the th with a weakness to yield to temptation. For the pro- ion of our company it has been necessary for us to make a at many arrests of boys ranging in age from ten to fifteen rs on the charge of theft and other offenses, and we have l, as you are aware, as many as fifteen and eighteen boys raigned in your Court on such charges at one time.

In a number of cases which we could cite of youths ar- sted by this department, whom we know had started on a ureer of crime, who received a suspended sentence in your ourt, and released on probation and required to report reg- larly to you regarding their future actions, have secured posi- ions and are leading better lives, with every indication of be- coming honorable men and good citizens.

While many of these youths are led into crime through poverty and pitiable circumstances realized by few, and cared for by less, and demonstrate vicious tendencies, many have never even had the assistance of a helping hand extended to them until taken into your Court charged with crime. Big hearts are in the breasts of most of these boys, and the fu- ture generations of families are at stake, and while we are obliged to arrest and prosecute them where the case justifies such action, we can not commend too highly the meritorious system you have adopted to check these boys in their down- ward career, and cause them to lead better lives.

The good effect your probation system is having among the boys of this city can be no better demonstrated than by the large decrease in the number of juvenile arrests this de- partment is required to make of such youthful offenders.

Yours respectfully,

W. H. RENO,

Superintendent Special Service.

OFFICE COLORADO & SOUTHERN RAILROAD.

Denver, Colo., January 11, 1904.

Hon. Ben B. Lindsey, County Judge, Denver, Colo.:

Dear Sir—A little over a year ago there appeared in your report of the Juvenile division of the county court a letter from the special service department of the Colorado & Southern Railway Company, noting the good results obtained through your method of handling minor offenders, a great number of whom this department brought before your honor for various acts perpetrated along the right of way and in the yards of the company.

As proof that your probation system is doing immense good, the youth with "swiping" inclination has troubled us less this past year than ever before, and our records show a marvelous decrease in the number of complaints filed as compared with the preceding year.

That your honor's efforts are being rewarded in the reformation of the froward child is evidenced by the fact that out of a court I know of only two of that number who wandered from the straight path while on probation and were rearrested, but I am glad to say have since reformed and regained the confidence of the community wherein they reside.

That parental indifference is greatly responsible for many a child's first lesson in stealing can be proven by any one familiar around railway yards. The children are sent and in many cases are driven to the yards to pick up coal and grain, which work they find slow and fatiguing, and to escape this and the scoldings surely awaiting them if they return home with empty sacks they steal from loaded cars, which means a repetition of the offense if once successful, and ultimately leading to committing more serious offenses as they grow older.

A case I recall to mind was tried in your court in October last and shows what effect prosecution and punishment has in cases of this kind. The mother, with her two sons, aged 10 and 12 years, were caught stealing several hundred pounds of coal, and to ascertain their poverty the officer followed them home. It was 6 o'clock in the morning, cold and frosty, and on arrival at the house the father, an able bodied, muscular fellow, was seated by a warm stove in the kitchen smoking, and in a contented manner watching the wreathes of smoke fading above his head. The family owned the cozy cottage they lived in and

onducted a vegetable garden near town; and investigation
ed that the father thought that the railroad company's
nen were in sympathy with and would not arrest women
hildren taking coal, whereas if he were caught pilfering
yards he would find his way to jail.

he result in this instance was that complaints were sworn
;ainst the whole family. The parents were reprimanded,
ghtly, too. The father was fined ten dollars, which has
tally put a stop to thieving in that section, and shivering
an are not seen skulking behind box cars in the frosty early
and at the instigation of thoughtless parents, waiting an
:unity to commit larceny.

'e think much good can yet be accomplished by giving
al attention to cases, as above narrated, as by pursuing
we reach the parents who directly are responsible for the
oning of their children into court.

have noticed in my attendance at the Juvenile court during
ar just closed such a marked improvement in the boy for-
looked upon as aspirant for the Reform School, that I
l the present system of correcting the erring child a god-
:o this community, and deserving the support and com-
.tion of all law-abiding citizens interested in the welfare
roper training of the unfortunate youth.

Respectfully yours,

.igned)   E. D. HEGG,
Special Service Department, C. & S. Ry.

E BUREAU OF CHILD AND ANIMAL PROTECTION.

Ben B. Lindsey,
   County Judge, Denver.

ear Sir:—The people of this city and State are fortunate
/ing a judge and a representative from the District At-
·'s office in his court wise enough to see that it is better
ze a child who has started wrong, start him right and
lim right till he grows into a good citizen, than it is to
n go wrong·till he grows into a vagabond or a criminal
len shut him up.

) dense is human stupidity that after many thousands
rs only a few people apparently have found this out yet.

Most of us still have faith in the jail as the best way to prevent wrong-doing, just as most of us still consider a blow and a curse the proper way to treat a dumb animal.

All things considered, the work being done by the Juvenile Department of the County Court in this city is the most important work being done by any court in the State, because it is more important to teach children to know and choose right from wrong, to ensure the welfare and happiness of whole life-times, than it is to impose penalties or decide property rights.

Yours very truly,
E. K. WHITEHEAD,
State Secretary.

ENDORSED BY SCHOOLS.

Superintendent's Rooms, Denver.

Hon. Ben B. Lindsey,
    Denver, Colorado.

Dear Sir:—It affords me much satisfaction to congratulate you and your Court upon the work of the Juvenile Division of the County Court, as I have had occasion to know about it during the past year. I am in hearty accord with the measures you have taken. Our Board of Education has appointed Mr. John J. Smith as School Attendance Officer for this district, and my relations with him have been so intimate and confidential during the past years that I have been made to know of his vigorous execution. I know of no influence so potent for relieving the municipal courts of the sad duty which has been theirs, of treating the young people as criminals, even before they have entered their teens. Your institution is avoiding that, and I trust that the power and influence of the schools, added to your own wise and fruitful enterprise, will continue, so that by the end of another year the truancies, already so much decreased, will be regarded as few, and our streets clear of loafing boys who are not criminal, but sure to become so unless they receive attention.

Perhaps it may be a matter of sentiment, but I would rather the officer of the Board of Education, to whom belongs those duties, be designated as School Attendance Officer, rather than Truant Officer. I have a notion that sometimes the stigma of an interview with the "Truant Officer" would be lessened if he were spoken of as the "School Attendance Officer;" yet, this is pure sentiment, and not, perhaps, practical.

Yours truly,
AARON GOVE,
Superintendent.

Superintendent's Rooms, April 19, 1904.

My Dear Judge Lindsey—I am very glad to learn that you have been nominated to succeed yourself in your present position and trust that your election will be uncontested. I am especially pleased at the very general expressions of approval of your work in connection with the Juvenile Court. It indicates that there is a growing realization on the part of the community that no effort to direct properly the development of our boys should be spared.

As superintendent in charge of school attendance I wish to express to you personally my appreciation of your earnest efforts to co-operate with the schools in securing more regular attendance at school, and your constant presentation to the boys that it is worth their while to do their very best in the school.

I think that one of the greatest results of the enforcement of the compulsory education act is the increasing realization upon the part of the community that the parent, except under extraordinary conditions, owes it to his children to at least secure for them an education equivalent to that obtained by the graduates of our grammar schools.

I firmly believe in the efficacy of the public schools as the best instrument for securing the social well-being of our community and gladly testify to the value of the service you render us through the operation of the Juvenile Court.

Very truly yours,
CHARLES E. CHADSEY.

PUBLIC SCHOOLS, DISTRICT No. 2.

L. C. Greenlee, Superintendent.

Hon. Ben B. Lindsey,
Denver, Colorado.

.Dear Sir:—I most heartily approve of the plan of probation or reporting system which you have established. Nothing has ever been done that will do more to save the young
boys from becoming criminals than your methods of dealing
with them. There is a vast improvement in the boys, and in
their parents as well. Some of them have taken a new lease
on life and have an idea of doing something and of making
something of themselves. Every boy in this town under the
age of twenty-one should be made to go to school or work.

Very truly yours,

L. C. GREENLEE.

In addition to the foregoing letters from the three superintendents of Denver schools, the Court has been honored by
letters from principals and teachers of the public schools, as
follows: Principals—Miss Eliza L. McGrew, Webster School;
R. H. Beggs, Whittier School; J. S. Eagleton, Harman School;
H. S. Phillips, Logan School; Dora M. Moore, Corona School;
L. P. Norvell, Washington School; Thomas B. Bird, Bryant
School; George B. Long, Swansea School; J. C. Stevens, Chel-
tenham School; Frona R. Houghan, Gilpin School; Essie Ed-
wards, Byers Street School; D. R. Hatch, Hyde Park School;
Charles A. Hollingshead, Columbian School; Martha A. Pease,
Delgany School; A. J. Flynn, Twenty-fourth Street School; H.
W. Zirkle, Elmwood School; Ed G. Arnold, Ebert School.
Teachers—L. B. Barnes, Genia H. Stillman, S. D. Allen, N. Mc-
Nany, Washington School; Alice T. Darlington, Elizabeth Rice,
M. L. Allen, Bryant School; Annie Kerr, Fannie E. Faris, Clara
E. Little, Delgany School; Fred Dick, of the Denver Normal
and Preparatory School.

Each of the letters referred to is an enthusiastic endorsement of the Juvenile Court and probation system, and only
lack of space prevents their publication.

THE COURT APPROVED.

(Colorado School Journal, May 9, 1904.)

e following resolution was passed by the Denver Teachers'
pril 12:

s citizens of Denver and teachers in her public schools,
ire to say, in regard to the work of Judge B. B. Lindsey
Juvenile Court:

'irst, that we believe that he is at work upon one of the
mportant problems now before the educational world.

iecond, that in our opinion his work has been an unqualified
s, of the greatest value to the cause of education in general
, the schools of Denver in particular.

Third, that we want him re-elected, believing that it would
public calamity if his work in the Juvenile department
l now lapse.

Resolved, that these statements be spread upon the min-
ind that a copy be sent to Judge Lindsey."

ROVAL BY THE PRESS.

The press of Denver and the entire State of Colorado has
itedly approved of the Juvenile Court and the work of its
e. Similar approval has come from the press gener-
in many States. A few of the editorials are here given
the four leading daily papers of Denver and weekly school
philanthropic journals, as illustrative of all:

HE IS A MASSEUR OF SOULS.

(Editorial Denver Post, December 15, 1903.)

Judge Ben B. Lindsey will be famous all over the world if
ieeps up his present lick in dealing with bad boys. His au-
ous stroke of sending incorrigibles to the Golden reform
iol, by themselves, illustrates his methods, which are to ex-
the boys' minds with a sense of personal responsibility.

What creates criminals of the vicious sort is the atrophy
he feeling of individual responsibility in the child. In a few
'u it will be too late; the sense of personal responsibility
be paralyzed beyond redemption. When that element is
'ned in a human being he is devoid of moral feeling and he
ipt straight only by fear of detection and punishment.

The boys who went to the reform school unguarded will not get over, in a hurry, the satisfaction of having kept their word of honor to the judge, even in taking themselves to jail. It was the first vigorous massage, as it were, of the boy's moral nerve. And doing this simple thing is really a great act, and Judge Lindsey's continued career as a masseur of souls will not go unheralded and unsung.

The criminal laws have been destroying boys' souls a long time. It has been an awful evil. And the world loves a man who is not afraid of his dignity in saving souls. What is the dignity of a pompous judge beside the value of a human being's moral sense that may be saved by a vigorous massage.

(Editorial Denver Times, April, 1904.)

Whoever else may or may not be elected at the approaching city election, Judge Lindsey should be chosen to succeed himself. So far as the public is informed of the intentions of the men who are in charge of affairs, it is understood to be the plan to leave Judge Lindsey off the Democratic ticket, whether it be a straight ticket or one nominated under fusion with the "antis."

Judge Lindsey is one of the men now holding office whose record entitles him to be kept there. His services to the community through the juvenile branch of the county court's work scarcely can be calculated.

If he is not nominated it will be as a punishment to him for the brave and straightforward exposure of the printing steal in which the old county ring was implicated. That very exposure, if he had done no other noteworthy thing, would be sufficient reason for his re-election.

If the Democratic convention commits the gross blunder of rejecting him it will be for his friends to bring his name before the public in some other way.

A GOOD NAME IS BETTER THAN GREAT RICHES.

(Editorial Denver Times, April, 1904.)

Judge Ben B. Lindsey has received the honor of a nomination upon both the Democratic and Republican tickets to succeed himself as county judge. It is the first time for nearly twenty years that the two parties have united in this State upon an important candidate, even for a judicial office.

Judge Lindsey stands before the people of the State as one of its truly great men, an eminence he has reached not by machine methods, not by deals or combinations, not by descent to devious or tricky manipulations, but by the force of integrity, by devotion to the highest ideals of citizenship, by strength of character and by tireless labor in the public interests. As a judge his record is spotless. As a citizen he dared to attack one of the most powerful political rings ever formed in this county and expose its corruption. As a judge he has united the citizen and the court in that work in behalf of juveniles which is peculiarly his own and which commands the approval and admiration of every thoughtful person. The effort in behalf of boys and girls and the laws under which such effort is possible are largely the outgrowth of Judge Lindsey's convictions on this subject. It was a work that had remained undone until he came upon the bench of the county court and which would have remained undone had he not taken it up.

The youth who stands at the threshold of life and contemplates the possibilities of a career sees before him many men of mark. He observes that most of them have gained prominence through the acquisition of wealth. But as he scrutinizes them more closely he finds that few indeed are without some blot. Very often their wealth has been gained by trampling others under foot, by fraud and sharp practice, by operations which may remain within the limits of the law, yet violate the spirit of equity and fair dealing. He sees that while such men have many to bow before them, yet they cannot be classed as great and good, and in his mind arises the ever-present question of whether true success may be gained by a mere race for wealth.

To such a youth the example of Judge Lindsey should be an inspiration. In the judge is seen a young man who has given his ability to the service of humanity and righteousness and who, in return, is honored by all; who is nearer and dearer to the people and enjoys more true respect and admiration than all the richest men of the State. The reputation of a Lindsey is a nobler achievement than the piling up of millions. It is a crown of manhood that money cannot buy. It is the tribute of the unerring instinct of the people to a man who is able and upright, who has the capacity to dream of great and splendid things and the energy and determination to do as well as to dream.

(Editorial Denver Republican, March 19, 1904.)

We direct attention to an article printed in this issue on the law compelling minors not engaged in some legitimate employment to attend school. It was written by Professor Aaron Gove and first printed in the March number of the Colorado School Journal.

In this article Professor Gove speaks in terms of the highest praise and strongest approval of the work done by Judge Lindsey in the effort to reclaim wayward boys, and more especially what he did toward securing the enactment of the law in question.

Professor Gove, as an educator and school superintendent of many years' experience, can speak with better knowledge than anyone else in this community in regard to the operation of such a law. He points out that while its enactment has added notably to the cost of conducting the schools in this and other large districts in the State, its effect must necessarily be beneficial. Practically it compels the authorities to take account of every minor in the school district, ascertaining why they are not at school, if they fail to attend, and forcing their attendance except where for legitimate reasons it may be excused.

The theory has often been advanced that it is better to spend money for schools rather than by neglecting the work of education to be compelled to increase the expenditure for jails and penitentiaries. Unfortunately, there is a percentage of children of school age who are not reached by the ordinary school laws. Hence arose the need of an enactment like the one which, largely through Judge Lindsey's influence, the legislature at its last session was induced to pass.

Professor Gove directs attention to the fact that while Judge Lindsey may in some cases go to extremes, his method of dealing with boys is, in the long run, in line with intelligent pedagogy, philosophy and humanity. That this is true seems to be beyond question to anyone who inquires carefully into what Judge Lindsey is doing. The cordial endorsement Professor

Gove has given his efforts in behalf of delinquent boys is gratifying to all of his friends.

The following editorial appears in the April number of Charities of New York:

If the children as well as the women could vote in Colorado there would not be any question of the re-election of one man. That man is Judge Ben B. Lindsey of the county court of Denver. The boys of the town would roll up a surprising majority for the boys' judge. The kids who have gathered around the big table in his chambers, the boys who have brought in more men for unlawfully selling liquor to minors—and brought them in by being "square"—than the police department had done in twenty years; the little fellow of 10 who held up another boy in an alley and robbed him of $3; the lad who led the raid on the bottled goods wagon and drank the stolen beer; the gang of boys who swiped things from back porches; "Mickey" and the others who joined forces in the fight against the jail which led to the starting of the detention home; the truant whose trouble was in his weak eyes and not in his bad heart, and the young rascal who was reformed by one touch of the surgeon's knife where forty thrashings had failed—and this because somebody at last was found who took enough interest in him to think out causes— these and a hundred others would muster up a mighty poll of strength. And there would be no question of the cleanness of this electorate, for these boys are of Denver's best, if youngest, citizenship to-day; friends and co-workers with the court and the learners of lessons in good government and the why of laws which are theirs because one judge did not forget that he had once been a boy; had come down from his bench and parleyed with them; had trusted them when others were too "wise;" had used their slang when their elders were not listening, and had crept into an understanding of their ways and the secret of building a whole man out of four-fifths of a boy, which all the law books and tomes and decisions in creation could not have afforded him.

The situation to-day is this: There is danger that the work stop, now that it is of most practical use locally and of most far-reaching influence in other States. Judge Lindsey will stand for re-election on May 15. That much is certain as this is written. Denver is peculiarly machine ridden at the present time. It happens to be the Democratic party now, but the situation is no worse than it used to be under the Republican party. Judge Lindsey has been tendered the nomination on the Democratic ticket, but on condition that he do certain things which he cannot and will not do. These things have nothing whatever to do with the treatment of children. The machine takes very little interest in the children. It is more concerned about jobs, and, unfortunately, there is a great deal of patronage connected with the county court. It is a civil and probate court as well as a children's court, doing the largest business of any court in the State—enough work, in reality, for three judges. There, then, is the rub. And unless there is recession from these demands on the part of the party leaders, Judge Lindsey will have to make the run independently, with the chances of fifty to one against him in the mind of the average bet-taker. But he will make the run, for in methods and make-up the man resembles District Attorney Jerome in New York and District Attorney Folk in St. Louis, friends of his, both of them, and fighters for decency all three.

Workers among children in other parts of the country are no better off than those boys of Denver. They cannot work in this May election. But they can bear witness to what it means that this missionary to boyhood—bad boyhood, if you will—be permitted to continue preaching his gospel. The Denver court began its work soon after the inauguration of the pioneer court in Chicago. Colorado today has the most comprehensive juvenile laws on the statute books of any State—a law which piecemeal legislation in half a dozen other States put together would not match, and a law which has been administered with less friction and more common sense than can be courteously used as units for comparison. These things must be known to citizens in Denver. Jacob Riis was there during the winter, and told them as much at some big meetings, for it was a Danish boy whom he made into an American. But it is natural that they do not know what store juvenile judges in other cities and child-saving workers generally lay on the continuance of the regime of this county judge. If the Missouri children's law is

upheld, as it was the past winter; if the Iowa legislature passes
a progressive juvenile court measure, as it did the past month;
if the common council of Atlanta passes an ordinance to similiar
effect, as it did the past fortnight—it is because in no small part
inspiration has been caught from the saner, surer, more wholesome methods of handling juvenile offenders which have been
worked to a head by a judge out in Denver.

(Editorial in the Juvenile Court Record, of Chicago. T. D.
Hurley, Editor.)

The watchword of the philanthropists interested in Juvenile
Court work has been, since the very inception of the idea, "A
Juvenile Court for every State in the country." While Illinois,
technically speaking, was the first State to provide a court
where juvenile defendants and delinquents could be dealt with
apart from adult criminals, nevertheless Colorado followed so
closely with a Juvenile Court that the two courts might truth-
fully be called "twin sisters in child-saving work."

The Denver Juvenile Court was brought about mainly
through the earnest efforts of Judge Benjamin B. Lindsey of that
city. For the past three years no one has been more persistent
in the practical, day-after-day spreading of the gospel of Juvenile
Court work than Judge Lindsey. Withal, his work has been
done so quietly that it is probable many of his fellow townsmen
do not realize the record he has made along the line. During
the past three years Judge Lindsey has made five speeches in
Michigan, one in New Jersey, two in New York, two in Missouri,
three in Kansas, at Lawrence and Topeka, two in Nebraska, three
in Georgia, three in Oregon, five in Washington, eleven in California and five in Iowa, on the subject of the work accomplished
by the Juvenile Court in saving young children from ultimate
lives of crimes. To this list should be added two church addresses in Chicago on the boy problem. Including the State of
Colorado, where, of course, Judge Lindsey is quite at home, and
where he has made seventy-six addresses on the subject, he has
carried the gospel of child saving into thirteen States, and has
made, in all, a total of one hundred and twenty speeches.

This outside work has never taken Judge Lindsey away from
his own court to exceed four weeks in any one year. As he has
not had a vacation for two years, it may be readily estimated how

indefatigable have been his efforts to persuade other States to take up the Juvenile Court idea. We do not believe there is another man or woman in the country who has done more along this line than Judge Lindsey.

The old saying that "a prophet hath no honor except in his own country" would seem to apply in this case, according to reports which have come to us. Judge Lindsey understands the Juvenile Court problem as few others in the country understand it. As Judge of the Denver Juvenile Court, he is the ideal man in the ideal place. No one else could take his place in the work and fill it as he does. Denver cannot afford to be without Judge Lindsey at the head of her Juvenile Court.

We trust the good people of Denver will bear this in mind when the 17th of May comes around, and will support him for re-election with such earnestness that there shall be no danger of another man being put in Judge Lindsey's place. We feel that it is only just to Judge Lindsey to call the attention of the citizens of Denver to the remarkable work he is doing as judge of the Denver Juvenile Court, and at the same time to remind them of the high opinion in which he is held by the best people throughout the country because of his efforts to raise up the fallen and to protect the weak, wherever possible, from falling at all.

A MAN WHO IS WORTH WHILE.

(Editorial Portland (Oregon) Journal, February, 1904.)

There is no man in the United States better qualified from practical experience, supplemented by gratifying success, to speak on the subject of a juvenile court and the treatment of delinquent children than Judge Ben B. Lindsey, who will address the people of Portland at the Unitarian church tonight.

The juvenile court over which he presides is now regarded as a model for all courts of like character. It found its starting point in finding the man. When he became county judge there was but a hodge-podge of contradictory and effete laws to govern the relations of the State to its delinquent children. Intensely interested in the question, intensely in earnest and very much more concerned with achieving results than slavishly following precedents, he set to work to build this branch of his labors from the ground up. At the start he had no intelligent laws to back him. Indeed, he was forced to take many things for granted and to give wide play to his common sense and experience. But it was not long before the public discovered that here was a real man; one who regarded his office not for the emoluments and dignities which went with it, but simply and solely as a means to an end, and that end to help the helpless to higher and better things. The work and the man had found each other, and not many months passed before he had on the statute books by unanimous legislative action every law that he required.

The law is no longer used in his court to make criminals of irresponsible children; it is administered to save them, to direct them along the right path, to extend the helping hand, to provide for them employment and to cover with the mantle of charity the backsliding that always comes in the earlier days of their reformation. This is part of the work upon which Judge Lindsey has been engaged, and the success which he has achieved is an inspiration to other workers in the same field who have striven vainly to better existing conditions. He is a man of heart and soul and feeling, a man who may dream his dreams, but who follows his plans upon intensely practical lines and achieves the most altruistic results from the most unpromising material and what to others might be the most discouraging succession of disappointments.

(Editorial Denver News, April 20, 1904.)

Judge Ben B. Lindsey was nominated by acclamation in the Republican convention, as he was nominated in the Democratic convention, to succeed himself as judge of the County Court. The double indorsement is a tribute to his work and to the strength of fearless, non-partisan honesty. It shows that a public officer who will do his whole duty, and something more, who is not afraid to stand forward and condemn corruption in his own party as well as in other parties, gains such tremendous strength that the politicians who prepare slates and make or mar candidates, dare not leave him off their tickets.

The young man who is dabbling in politics will do well to profit by the career of Judge Lindsey, which demonstrates that the best and greatest success comes from fearless performance of duty.

(Colorado School Journal.)

The law concerning the attendance of children at school which became effective over the signature of the Governor at the close of the last legislature, is one of the most notable and important that the State has ever passed relating to education. It has turned over to school boards a duty and a responsbility scarcely ever equaled. In the larger school districts of the State the expense for the execution of this law is material, thereby increasing the cost of the conduct of schools. Few citizens can appreciate immediately the effects of such a contemplated revolution in securing the care and preservation of such young people in the State as have irresponsible homes, from the temptations to criminal life. So far as I know, no law has ever been enacted as sweeping and· complete. A revolution of this kind cannot be effective in a short time, but the outcome ultimately is sure to be such as will redound to the good name of Colorado and Colorado schools. The history of this movement, if it were written, would present the effort and energy of one of the foremost men in the cause, Judge Lindsey of the Denver county court.

The organization and direction of a school attendance department in cities like Denver, Colorado Springs and Pueblo, adds a material duty to the superintendent's department. This earnest and faithful advocate, Judge Lindsey, has worked with extraordinary vigor along the line of prevention of crime rather than punishment of crime, and this, his measures are bound to accomplish. Whatever criticisms are made as to this reform in the community, are largely from lack of information. It must be remembered that every ardent advocate of a good measure, since the foundation of the world, has been subjected to criticism and abuse chiefly on account of extreme positions. Judge Lindsey, from the very force of his heart and head, may occasionally take an extreme position, but in the long run it will be found that the advice which he gives and the practices which he follows, in refraining from awarding the punishment that belongs to the adult criminal to the youthful criminal, is along the line of intelligent pedagogy, philosophy and humanity. The educational forum has from the beginning talked of the economy of administration in the State by spending money for schools rather than for jails and penitentiaries. But there has ever been too large a percentage of young people who could not be reached by the ordinary public school, and this law of which Judge Lindsey is the promoter and for the passage of which he labored so earnestly, it will be seen, in the first place, provides for the employment of a force that will require the accounting for the conduct of every minor in the school district, and, secondly, compelling the minor to be legitimately and respectably at work, or, what is better in all ordinary cases, to be at school.

It is somewhat surprising that this law and the efforts made for its execution have so far attracted so little attention, but little by little in every community the attention of the people will be called to the minority of irresponsible fathers who live without regard to parental responsibilities, and who, it is trusted, will be made to know that there is a God in Israel and that one of his lieutenants with regard to the protection of youth is named Ben B. Lindsey.   AARON GOVE.

Professor Gove has been for thirty years superintendent of Denver schools and is one of the most eminent educators in America.

LETTERS FROM BOYS.

The trust and confidence in boys and the interest taken in them by the Juvenile Court, brings a large correspondence with boys. Judge Lindsey receives and answers hundreds of letters from them each year. Some of his best friends and most regular correspondents are the boys whom he has sent to the State Industrial School. One of the first boys the Judge ever sent to the Industrial School was one of these. He was sent because of no home and exceptional circumstances. He had been, without the knowledge of the Court, kept in jail several weeks before brought to court. The letter from the boy first caused the Judge to resolve to smash the jail for "little kids," and in the end it was smashed, for it would cost an officer $100 fine to put the same boy there again. A part of the letter follows:

A BOY'S OPINION OF JAIL LIFE AND THE INDUS-TRIAL SCHOOL.

"This school is a good deal different from what I was afraid it would be when I was sent here. I had been in the Arapahoe County Jail, with all its locks and bars and gates, and got the impression that all places for boys were as stern and gloomy. A jail ought to be for criminals that can be kept nowhere else. I had committed no crime when I was taken to the jail, and I felt badly when they turned the key and locked me in, and I looked around and saw bars all around me. There was nothing to remind me of good things and I felt homesick and discouraged. When I got to this school I was surprised to see such nice, clean rooms, with everything so neat and home-like. Our dormitory was so much different from the old place where we had to sleep when in jail. But I never can forget that I was shut in from the beautiful flowers and trees that I had left outside when the door clanged behind me. Only a little spot of the sky could be seen, and that looked strange when seen through iron bars. I though of the little birds I used to put in a cage and I determined to never pen up a wild creature again. When I came here the boys all seemed so contented and happy that I wondered if they had had the same experience that I had. Some boys say that they don't care, fo they have been in jail anyway, and twice is not much worse than once. I don't feel that way, and I think that all boys feel very badly the first time they are locked in a jail. This is the first letter that I ever wrote on a typewriter.

"Your loving friend,

"_____ _____."

Age, 12.

These letters would form an interesting volume of themselves, and with the history of some of the writers would make a story of absorbing interest. But owing to the length of this chapter no attempt is made to publish any of them.

LETTERS FROM PARENTS.

A great many letters from parents are received at the Juvenile Court during the year, expressing appreciation and gratitude, and though some of the best are here given, they illustrate the spirit of all:

Denver, Colo., March 9, 1904.

Hon. Ben B. Lindsey, Judge of County Court:

Dear Sir and Friend—While I am a comparative stranger to you I feel that I may so address you without offense. You have befriended me and mine. You have kept a stain from the family name. Your words have been those of a father. Your conduct has been as tender as that of a mother. You have been firm, but gentle, in your words. There are no stings. The Juvenile Court, over which you preside, is doing a great work. My son loves and respects you. I believe that his heart, like mine, is filled with a gratitude unspeakable. If anything will make a man of a wayward youth you have found the way. The wisdom that corrects an error and commends a virtue, that justice which has within it a heart-throb, a pulsation of pity, a tempering of mercy, appeals to a higher civilization and bespeaks a beautiful future.

I feel that I could not make a suggestion to one who has given his life to the work and has gone to the very bottom of the greatest subject of modern inquiry, "The treatment of juvenile offenders." Thanking you for myself and family, I have the honor to be,　　　　Gratefully yours,

Denver, Colo., March 10, 1904.

Hon. Ben B. Lindsey, Judge Juvenile Court, Denver, Colorado:

Dear Judge—Having been a deputy sheriff of this county in former years, I think I can appreciate very sharply the humanitarian advantages of the new over the old way of exercising juvenile control.

The conduct of my boy, H., 14 years old, is almost exemplary since coming under the influence of your methods and procedure, regarding habits, obedience and hours, and is in happy contrast to his former irregularities in many particulars.

My information is that other parents are enjoying the comforts of the change of systems, equally with ourselves.

With personal good wishes and thanks, I bespeak for you prosperity and progression in the work. I remain,

Yours very respectfully,

Denver, Colo., March 8, 1904.

To Judge Lindsey:

Dear Sir—Our son Charles was brought to your court through thoughtlessness, being led by others, etc. I felt very much humiliated; labored under the impression that the law would hold the child responsible for his error and charge him with crime.

I feared that such severe measure would harden the child and blight his future forever. The idea of being numbered among criminals and to bear the reproach would cause any sensitive child to lose self-respect and lead it astray. Of course, we all know that love without severity is moral weakness. But I must say that I was deeply impressed when I saw your wise way in reasoning with the child; pointing out to him his mistake and what the result would be should he continue to do wrong, etc. I certainly appreciated the way you tempered your judgment with mercy. "Go and sin no more." It has taught the child a lifelong lesson never to be forgotten, to avoid the very appearance of evil. He has formed a high regard for Judge Lindsey for saving him from being disgraced and taunted by his companions, etc.

The child knows where his heart is at rest, where a palliating, protecting, tender, loving, forgiving care surrounds his every act and deed; the spot where he is safe, housed against an unkind world whose tender mercies are cruel, "the home where his mother presides." I always taught the child how severe the law is with those who err, etc., hence he greatly feared, but his heart rejoiced at Judge Lindsey's kind consideration in pardoning his mistake, etc., and putting him on probation for a time. It caused him to take more heed to his ways, approving things that are excellent, and to be more sympathetic towards others, etc. Sympathy is one of the great secrets of life. It overcomes evil and strengthens good. It disarms resistance, melts the hardened heart, and develops the better part of human nature.

Kindly accept our hearty thanks for the benefit received from the Juvenile Court. Very respectfully,

Denver, Colo., March 9, 1904.

Mr. B. B. Lindsey:

Dear Sir—I think John has been doing fine since he has been reporting at your court. I think there ought to be more of those courts like yours and boys would not get in so much trouble. John pays his own car fare down town when he goes to see you. He likes to report. It helps him so much that he don't care so much for running with the boys.   Yours truly,

Denver, Colo., March 27, 1904.

Judge Lindsey:

Dear Sir—Henry was not a bad boy, but he did try hard to be excuced from your court, and I hope he will not cause you any further trouble. My opinion is that your court is doing a great deal of good, and I hope you will help the boys all you can. They are not so bad as some make them, and may God help them. Some of them have poor homes. One thing I say and that is that the police do run down the boys for little reasons. If they would be more kind to them we would have better boys. I think when a boy works all days and happens to stop to talk with another boy he ought not to be run down by a policeman. So I will close, hoping that Henry will be good in the future.

From your friend,

DENVER'S JUVENILE COURT JUDGE.

(From Denver Post, December 31, 1903.)

Benjamin Barr Lindsey was born on a farm near Jackson, Tenn., thirty-four years ago. His father located in Denver in 1878. He attended the public schools of Denver when a boy. In 1885 he returned to his birthplace, his grandfather's farm at Jackson, where he spent two or three years of his boyhood. At the age of sixteen the ill health of his father required his return to Denver. Shortly after his return his father died. He was the eldest of four children, and the burden of responsibility for the support of the family, including his mother, devolved upon him. He was aided by one of his younger brothers, Chalmers A. Lindsey. In 1888 he entered the law office of Hon. R. D. Thompson in the capacity of office boy. To this he added other duties, such as carrying a newspaper route in the mornings and doing janitor work at nights, and at the same time devoting his spare time to the study of law. He remained with Mr. Thompson for eight years, succeeding to the position of clerk in that office and general assistant. In 1896 he formed a partnership with Senator Fred. W. Parks under the firm name of Lindsey & Parks. This relation successfully continued until January, 1901, when he became County Judge, as successor to Hon. Robert W. Steele, who had resigned in consequence of his election to the supreme bench. In 1900 he was engaged by the Democratic party as counsel in the numerous election cases that arose under the Australian ballot system, which at that time occasioned much litigation between contending factions of the Democratic party as to the right to claim party name, party emblem, etc. In the Democratic convention in the fall of 1900 he came within fifteen votes of being nominated as a candidate for District Judge. At that time he was less than thirty years of age.

Since he became County Judge he has been responsible for many innovations. At his suggestion a State County Judges' Association was formed, which in a brief year has accomplished a revision of all the probate laws of the State into a probate code, making many corrections in the old law and adding rights to widows and orphans which theretofore had not existed.

The most important public work which has engaged his services upon the county bench has been in behalf of more advanced and intelligent methods of dealing with children offenders through the Juvenile Court. He is the author of the Juvenile Court laws and important amendments to the school laws and the child labor laws of Colorado. His work in this direction has attracted national attention.

He has delivered addresses in eight or ten States upon his favorite topic of the children's laws. Recently he delivered such an address at the State conference of Charities and Corrections of Missouri, and the Memphis Commercial Appeal referred to the matter, editorially, under the title of "Young Tennesseeans Abroad," as follows: "By a noteworthy coincidence the two principal speakers selected are young Tennesseeans, both hailing from the western division of the 'Old Volunteer' State. The names of the young men in question are Joseph W. Folk of St. Louis and Benjamin Lindsey of Denver. Folk is a

9

native of Brownsville and Lindsey is from Jackson, towns sep-
arated by a distance of twenty-seven miles. Both are lawyers
and both have won fame for their fearless defense of civic
purity.

"Tennesseeans, irrespective of party lines, doubtless will
feel a pleasurable interest in the honor conferred upon Messrs.
Folk and Lindsey, and see in their distinction a glory reflected
upon the State which cradled and nurtured them, and in whose
institutions the mind of each was shaped and fitted for careers
signally honorable.

"Joe Folk is a national figure, because of the size of the
battles he has fought and won and the prominence of the field
over which he has maneuvered.

"Judge Lindsey, as he is known in the Rockies, for he is
serving his third year as County Judge, has fought valiantly,
but his operations have covered a smaller area of territory than
the young St. Louisan's, and the result of his victories have
been felt in a community more removed from the great throb-
bing center of population."

Judge Lindsey lives with his mother in Denver. He has
had the care of a family since a boy himself, in which was his
younger brother of three years old, whom he has raised and
cared for, and as he says himself, he has been so busy caring
for one family and helping to care for and correct the children
of hundreds of others, he is still single. He is active in every
good work for the city and has been uncompromising in de-
nouncing and exposing corruption in politics in Denver, having
thereby incurred some bitter enemies politically, but a host
of friends among the people, as a result of which he ran several thousand votes ahead of his ticket in the election of 1901,
and received an almost unanimous vote (55,000) at the Denver
election in May, 1904.

Statement of Civil and Probate
Divisions of County Court

REPORT OF CIVIL AND PROBATE DIVISIONS OF COUNTY COURT FOR 1903.

Civil cases filed.. 1,439
Probate cases filed...................................... 625

Total cases filed.................................... 2,064
Trials to court, or jury............................... 707
Civil orders entered in court.........................11,214
Probate orders, including appointment of executors, administrators, guardians, proof of wills, settling estates, adoptions and lunacy trials entered in court... 9,440

Total number of orders...........................20,654
Total pages of record transcribed in books.............. 9,275

INCOME AND EXPENDITURES OF THE COUNTY COURT FOR THE YEAR 1903.

Earnings for the twelve months from January 1, 1903,
to December 31, 1903...........................$22,786.86
Expenses for the same period for judge's salary and
clerical hire 18,066.23

Excess of earnings for 1903.....................$ 4,720.63
Due and uncollected from the city and county as a litigant for 1903................................. 1,011.56

Total earnings for 1903.......................$ 5,702.19
Average monthly expense for judge's and clerks' salaries for 1903................................. 1,505.52

During the year 1903 there was turned over to the treasurer $10,000, out of the surplus earnings of this office, and in addition the further sum of $1,374.05 for jury fees, making a total of $11,374.05 placed in the treasury of the City and County of Denver to the credit of this court.

STATEMENT OF CIVIL AND PROBATE DIVISIONS OF COUNTY COURT FROM JANUARY 1, A. D. 1901, TO DECEMBER 31, A. D. 1903 (three years).

Civil cases filed.................................... 3,773
Probate cases filed.................................. 1,974

Total cases filed................................. 5,747
Trials to court, or jury............................. 2,125
Civil orders entered in court........................24,724
Probate orders, including appointment of executors, administrators, guardians, proof of wills, settling estates, adoptions and lunacy trials entered in court..22,742

Total number of orders..........................47,466
Total pages of record transcribed in books.............23,897

Earnings from Jan. 8, 1901, to Dec. 31, 1903..........$66,481.63
Expenses from Jan. 8, 1901, to Dec. 31, 1903.......... 52,523.20

$13,958.43

Not included in this item is the amount due from the City and County of Denver as a litigant for its November and December business 1,011.56

Total surplus earnings, Jan. 8, 1901, to Dec. 31, 1903..$14,969.99
Average monthly earnings from Jan. 8, 1901, to Dec. 31, 1903 .... 1,846.71
Average monthly expense for judge's salary and clerical hire from Jan. 8, 1901, to Dec. 31, 1903...... 1,458.87
Number of letters written to boys..................... 295

THOS. L. BONFILS,
Clerk of the County Court of Denver, Colorado.

Index

INDEX.

Frontispiece, Hon. Ben. B. Lindsey, Judge of the Juvenile
    Court ....
Foreword 3
What the Judge Thinks of the Work................. 7

CHAPTER I.

The Fight for Childhood—Youth and Crime.......... 15

CHAPTER II.

The Law and the Court 23
The Juvenile Law and Court 25
Probation 25
New Features of Law 25
Summary Chart of All Charges during the years 1901-
    1902-1903 26
Summary Chart of All Commitments for the years 1901-
    1902-1903 27
Illinois Law 28
Colorado Laws 28
The Work and the Law 29
Advantages of Juvenile Law 29
True Function of State 29
The Law in Denver and Colorado 30
Probation Chart, showing the totals in round numbers on
    the left, percentages on right..................... 31
Objections to Juvenile Law 32
The Court and the Home 34
Treatment of Child Offenders 34
Criminal Court and Juvenile Court compared 35
The Present Colorado Law and the Details of its Operation
Delinquency 37
The Compulsory School Law 38
Dependent Children 39
The Law and the Court 40
Preparation of Law 40
Special Features of Colorado Law 40
Paid Probation Officers 40
How Appointed 41
The Expense of Probation 41
Powers of Probation Officer 43

How Complaints are Filed 43
The Fee System of Paying Officers 44
Powers of Court Not Abused 44
How Law Extends to Entire State 45
The Law is Elastic and Valid 45
Exceptional Cases 46
Children and Parent Cases All in One Court 46
Due Process of Law—Jury Trial, Right to Counsel, etc... 47
Annual Report from Courts 48
Detention School 48
Correct the Child But Protect the Child 50
Arm of Discipline 50
How Boys Are Trusted 50
Commitments and Institutions 51
Religious Instructions 51
Adopted into Homes 51
Construction of Law 53
Adult Delinquency Law—Parents and Others Responsible. 53
Some Interesting Cases in Point...................... 54
On the Tracks and Stealing Coal..................... 54
Careless Parents 55
Sending Children to Evil Places..................... 55
A Twelve-Year-Old Thief............................. 55
A Check on Boy Bums................................ 57
Probation of Men and Women for Faults of the Child.. 57
The Messenger Company and the Boys............... 58
The Evils of Street Employment—The Power of Example 58
Compulsory Education and How the School Helps...... 59
Special Features of School Law...................... 60
Exemption 60
School Attendance Officers.......................... 61
Parental School 61
School Law Enforcement............................. 62
Child Labor Law.................................... 63
Enforcement of Child Labor Law......................63
Child Labor and Compulsory Education.............. 64
Impracticable Features of Child Labor Law Remedied.. 65
Work and Play...................................... 66
Wisdom of Child Labor Laws........................ 66
Summary of Laws 67

CHAPTER III.

Administrative Work................................ 71
Two Classes of Boys................................ 71
Girls 71
Why We Get Reports................................ 72
Average Boys and Difficult Boys..................... 73
Saturday Morning Talks............................. 74

Subjects of the Talks.............................. 75
Slang Terms....................................... 77
The Word of Cheer................................. 78
Objections to Report Sys'.m....................... 79
Difficulties of Report Syst.m..................... 80
How the Schools Work With the Court............... 80
How the Causes Come Out in the Grind.............. 81
The Physician and the Court....................... 82
Pure Cussedness................................... 83
Skill Required.................................... 83
The Teacher and the Boy........................... 84
The Attendance Officer and the Probation Officer 85
Reports of Working Boys. 85
Employers and Employment 85
Reports During School Vacation 87
Time of Probation and Rules 88
Classification of Cases 88

I.

Mischievous Children 89
How the Home and the School Helps 90
How the City and the Country Boys Differ.......... 90
Court Necessary in Mischievous Cases.............. 90
All To Be Treated Alike 90
Mischievous Cases Easily Corrected 91
Boys Best Help in Mischievous Cases............... 92

II.

Children Who Are Too Weak To Resist Temptation 92

III.

Children Victims of Incompetent Parents 93
Too Much Ease, Money and Good Time................ 93
Bad Examples 94
Lack of Companionship 95
Railroad Cases 95
Proof that Parents Are to Blame................... 95
Juvenile Anarchists 96

IV.

Environment and Association 96
What To Do 97

V.

Boy Bums and Runaways 98
Causes 99

Lax Enforcement of the Laws Intended for the Protection
of Children 99
Divorce, Desertion, Drink and, of Course, Damnation of
the Home 100
Cases Classified, Causes Considered 100
Baths and Literature 100
The Gang 101
How the Case Against the Child Must Be Judged....... 104
How the Juvenile Court Works with the Boys and the Boys
with the Court 106
Element of Interest in a Boy's Life 106
How Boys Enforce the Law 107
Get the Truth 108
Legal Technicalities Avoided by the Juvenile Court 109
Where the Criminal Law Fails 109
How the Truth Saved the Boy 110
A Case That Almost Failed 113
Troubles of Children 114
Not Afraid To Be Caught 114
How the Boys Regard the Court 115
Employment Bureau 115
Visitation by Probation Officers 116
Parents' Meetings 116
School Principals' Meetings 116
Increase in Juvenile Delinquency 117
Children Better Cared For 118
How the Case Grows 118
The Snitching Bee 118
How the Dragnet Works 118
A Positive Decrease in Juvenile Offenses in Denver......119
Truancy Decreasing 120
Trust and Confidence in Boys 120
Boys Go To Jail and Industrial School Alone...........120
Who the Boys Are 121
If We Should Fail.................................121
The Purpose of the Plan 121
Needy Children Relieved 122
A Case in Point 122
Lack of Nourishment 123
The Fight Against the Jail 124
The True Function of the Juvenile Court 125
The Judge of the Juvenile Court 125
The Work Important 126
Juvenile Court Only a Part of the System 127
Do Not Expect Too Much—Test of Success 127
The Juvenile Improvement Association 127
Work in the Beet Fields 129

Success in the Best Fields 131
Boys' Clubs 133
Recommendations as Preventatives of Delinquency 133
1st. Use of Schools 133
2nd. Ungraded Rooms. Industrial Work 133
3rd. Play Grounds 134
4th. Parents' Meetings 134
5th. Detention School 134
6th. Juvenile Betterment 134
7th. Enforce Laws 134
8th. School Attendance 135
9th. Co-operation 135
10th. Police Department 135
11th. Work by Teachers 136
12th. Records and Assistance 136
13th. Mutual Helpfulness 137
Those Who Have Helped 137
Why Help Is Needed in the Court 139
What the Boys Say 142

CHAPTER IV.

Facts and Figures 151
Disposition of Dependent Cases 151
Forms of Delinquency Charged 151
Ages of Delinquents 151
Disposition of Delinquents 152
Causes of Crimes 152
Report System Adopted by this Court 153
Record of Probations for 1901-1902-1903 154
Voluntary Delinquents and Probationers 154
Total Number of Children Dealt With in the Juvenile
    Court During the Years 1901-1902-1903 154
Literature Distributed Each Month 155
Ages of Delinquents, 1901-1902-1903 158
Monthly Reports by Probation Officers 158
Probation Officer's Report for February, 1904 159
Probation Officer's Report for March, 1904 160
Probation Officer's Report for April, 1904 161
Probation Officer's Report for May, 1904 162

CHAPTER V.

The Expense 165
Money Invested in Jails in Denver 167
Annual Expenditure for Maintenance of Jails and Crim-
    inal Courts in Denver 167
Comparison of Expense and Results Obtained Under Old
    System and the Present 170

The Case of One Boy 172
Comparative Tables of Expense......................173
Summary 177
Detention House 177
Annual Expense 177
Saving in Expense to City, County and State for Three
    Years by Juvenile Court 178
Some Deductions 178
Expensive Boys 180

CHAPTER VI.

The Court Approved 181
Political Approval of the Juvenile Court 183
Public School Indorsement 193
Aproval by the Press 194
Letters from Boys 204
Denver's Juvenile Court Judge 208
Report of Civil and Probate Divisions of County Court for
    1903 213
Statement of Civil and Probate Divisions of County Court
    from January 1, 1901, to December 31, 1903. (Three
    Years.) 214

Lightning Source UK Ltd.
Milton Keynes UK
UKHW010214271118
332995UK00015B/1870/P